Praise for

Insufficient Rewards

Insufficient Rewards: How We Traded Integrity for Comfort and Outsourced Morality to History is a unique look at how we view and process history, written from a moral philosophical lens. It's particularly relevant for current times, where our ideological and political polarization has gone off the rails and historical illiteracy is devastating informed discourse. Jay has astutely and cleverly picked out patterns and precedents we can all learn from that I haven't seen written about anywhere else — and he writes in a really engaging, playful way that had me going, "Oh, now I get it!" more than a few times.
Ali A. Rizvi, Canadian physician, writer, activist

Insufficient Rewards

How We Traded Integrity for Comfort and Outsourced Morality to History

Insufficient Rewards

How We Traded Integrity for Comfort and Outsourced Morality to History

by Jay Shapiro

IFF
BOOKS

London, UK
Washington, DC, USA

CollectiveInk

First published by iff Books, 2026
iff Books is an imprint of Collective Ink Ltd.,
Unit 11, Shepperton House, 89 Shepperton Road, London, N1 3DF
office@collectiveinkbooks.com
www.collectiveinkbooks.com
www.iff-books.com

For distributor details and how to order please visit the 'Ordering' section on our website.

ISBN: 978 1 80341 998 5 (Paperback)
978 1 917991 13 1 (ebook)
Library of Congress Control Number: 2025940665

A CIP catalogue record for this book is available from the British Library.

Design: Lapiz Digital Services

UK: Printed and bound by CPI Group (UK) Ltd, Croydon, CR0 4YY
Printed in North America by CPI GPS partners

The manufacturer's authorised representative in the EU for product safety is:
eucomply OÜ - Pärnu mnt 139b-14, 11317 Tallinn, Estonia,
hello@eucompliancepartner.com,
www.eucompliancepartner.com

Contents

Preface

The human condition is a wrestling match between comfort and conscience. This book aims to understand that tension and the unstable world which is continuously birthed from and broken by our capacity to think morally.

This book is my attempt to explain the strange moment we're in. It feels like a slow, heavy slide into malaise, but also like we're just one spark away from revolution or collapse. The idea of "insufficient reward" is the lens I use to understand it. More and more people are stuck in a zone where the world asks for their loyalty, patience, and belief in progress, but offers only alienation, contradiction, and a creeping sense of betrayal. Some stay frozen in that tension, justifying a system that quietly erodes them. Others snap out of it, reject the offer entirely, and start pushing for something else. This split isn't just a mood or a trend. It is the emotional foundation of our current world, and it helps explain why everything feels so stuck and so volatile at the same time.

In these pages I will dismantle the treacherous seesaw of moral frameworks we've all been stuck on, the one ridden by rigid deontological principle-preachers on one end and infinitely flexible utilitarian rationalizers on the other. In its place, I outline a more grounded and humane way to evaluate our moral lives and the political systems we generate. I offer a thorough examination of the tenuous state of things, but unlike many other familiar critiques, I argue that ours is a world not in tragic *crisis* but in hopeful *revolt* against a forced trade-off of our moral integrity, one that can only ever deliver rewards of infinite insufficiency.

This *is* an optimistic book. Believe it or not, those still do exist, and they are written from time to time, even by people like me who have more than a few concerns. The optimism which is woven through the paragraphs is not the type which guesses, predicts, or promises that things will be "peaceful," "stable," or necessarily "better." It is a different type of optimism which discovers pride and encouragement deeply embedded in the very same psychological tension which is generating so much of the volatility and horror.

This is an admittedly ambitious book. But we find ourselves living in a world deteriorating in moral atrophy and retreat, a moment that demands ambition. And we are, I insist, in spite of the many naysayers, capable of the task of moral transcendence.

My aim is threefold. First, to expose and parse the reasons behind the widespread conflation of technological progress with moral progress, a confusion that sits at the root of the divide between liberalism and leftism. Second, to locate and define moral integrity as the existentially sacred value we have been coerced to trade away for rewards that are, in the end, inherently insufficient. And third, to dismantle and ultimately reject the submissive, pseudo-religious habit of invoking "history" as both an unquestioned archive of moral lessons and a kind of external judge. That third aim runs through the entire book, as I explore the many ways we deflect our own moral agency by outsourcing judgment to the past or future, as if history could absolve us of the decisions that still belong to us.

What you are holding is not a "history book," but rather, a moral philosophy book "concerned with history." Though, in the process of writing and researching, I have encountered fascinating historical accounts and narratives. I'm excited to share some with you. It is tempting to gush for chapters on end about the characters, moments, and monuments that I have researched. I will refrain from doing so, but I hope this book sparks love and hunger for history in you in the same way it has in me.

I will trace the psychological and philosophical origins of our very strange relationship with the concept of "history" to its roots: our longing for moral certainty and obligation, our prayers for divine authority, and our desperate seeking of relief from the painful freedom of being a moral creature capable of counterfactual moral universe comparison. This flight from freedom comes in many forms of nominating others, or our splintered selves, to carry the burden of moral violation for our truest selves.

If I'm successful, you will not only be able to think about morality more clearly, decipher political debate more lucidly, and understand your own moral frustrations more transparently, but you will also enjoy a deeper and more thoughtful experience when strolling through a museum, leafing through a family photo album, or even scrolling through the insanity of our digital news landscapes.

This is how I've come to upgrade my understanding of "history" through clearer moral thinking: history, that unwieldy thing of the past, is not a settled record or a fixed picture. *It is the ambiguous and arbitrary medium in which moral decisions are made.*

The arguments made within these pages narrate how the tension between that *time-bound* contextual moral truth and our simultaneous yearning for objective, *timeless* moral instruction becomes the unstable and nervous fault line for so much of our trouble, both personally and politically.

Yes, this book takes critical aim at many of the assumptions baked into modern life, and notably what we have come to call "The West," but it is not a rejection or denial of important forms of scientific progress. It is a call to interrogate the word "progress" itself, an invitation to ask what forms of it we ought to value and which ones have been eclipsed and intentionally erased or suffocated.

You will come to see just how skeptical I am of utilitarian frameworks focused on "maximizing flourishing" and "minimizing suffering." But I am obviously not opposed to "flourishing." I simply want to challenge the assumptions of the term and to better understand the necessary components of it, in particular the most difficult and inconvenient flourishing ingredient of them all: justice.

This is a book which seeks to point toward worlds worth winning and steer us clear of worlds which are merely false impressions of them, no matter how technologically seductive, politically stable, nominally peaceful, or physically safe. It won't surprise you much after reading the subtitle to discover that I think we have built a world very much like that.

There are no easy answers in this book. Sorry.

I view my role as an author of philosophy and storyteller to complicate the picture whenever we become too certain or comfortable. My job is to tell someone, and myself, that they probably have been asking a bad question if they think they've found the final answer. So, we're going to be dealing with a lot of big questions that might not even *have* answers. I will try to convince you that this exquisite torture is much more fun than it sounds. I will likely not *fully* succeed. I am still working on convincing myself of that folly.

I will parse the tasks of the journalist, the historian, and the philosopher when it comes to situating our moral selves. I will examine their roles in constructing, interpreting, and ultimately challenging our understanding of what *has* happened, what *could have* happened, and what *should have* happened. We will see how their interrelated processes inevitably construct morally laden narratives which morph into the means of collective remembering. And we will unfortunately see how many of these narratives are deployed to justify certain moral nightmares of the status quo under the sledgehammer-like claims of necessity or collateral damage.

Ultimately, this book casts a wide analytical, psychological, and philosophical net on the human condition in an effort to understand what is *really* fueling the noisy reckoning of our time. This understanding can only be found by diving deeply into the fragile and vulnerable relationships between ourselves, each other, our existential isolation, our moral madness, our constructed historical narratives, and our imagined legacies. And dive we will.

So, if you've been feeling an unshakable discomfort you can't quite place, something that both excites and terrifies you, a sense that the world is cracking open and you're not sure whether to hold it together or help it crumble, don't worry, that's not a glitch. That's just your moral integrity trying to get a word in. This book will help you listen to it and to recognize the fleeting opportunity to respond, before someone or something else does it for you. And in the process of learning how to intervene in our internal moral conversations, we might just change "history."

Introduction

This Book Has a Villain

Why the voice in your head wants you to stop reading, and why that's a very good sign

The World in ~~Crisis~~ Revolt

This book's title comes from a landmark finding in psychology: when people accept a reward that is too small to justify a clear moral violation, they often don't rebel. Instead, they revise their internal desires and beliefs in order to erase the sense that a violation occurred at all. I'll be making the case that the façade of this global psychic architecture, though remarkably strong and stable, has been pushed to its limits by a world hypnotized by a thin conception of progress and the building is beginning to crack.

Briefly, it works like this. When we suffer from clashing values and feel the jamming of moral gears in our minds, we automatically look for escape from the unbearable condition. We seek blissful equilibrium. And when we are lured to this safety by rewards that we *know* to be "insufficient," we find a novel way out of the mess. We rewrite our own historical narrative. We alter our reality, memory, and even our beliefs and preferences with a revised story that gets the gears moving smoothly again. That's how the mind resolves the pain of contradiction. It patches over the dissonance with lies that become beliefs.

This is not a new condition for man. But we've certainly been doing *a lot* of it lately, and it's been strengthening in its intensity, worsening in terms of costly repairs, and spreading into nearly all aspects of life. The relentless patchwork has worked its way into the deepest grooved paths of how we think, work, vote, apologize, hope, kill, love, parent, eat, and more. And the labor of all this mental repair work is wearing us down into malaise or madness. It is sometimes difficult to distinguish those.

We're told that this feeling is just the residue of our bold voyage into the future, part of some grand civilizational story of growth and progress. But there's a nagging truth hitched to the hull of that ship like a gangly barnacle. This book is about dealing with that barnacle. And hidden in that grim image is genuinely good news.

If we can recognize how fragile and panicked this epidemic of deep rationalization really is, we might stop treating it like an inevitability, a "necessary trade-off," or a form of collateral damage. We might start seeing it for what it is, a nervous reflex born out of our existential fear of freedom and our burdensome capacity for moral world imagination and creation. Don't worry, we'll have time to untangle all of that. But the important part to note now is that beneath the paradoxical anxious malaise so many of us are feeling, the human spirit is still kicking. The purely secular prayer, the existential desire for cosmic belonging, the unshakable feeling of containing divine dignity, and the relentless pulse of moral integrity are all still there. Restlessly stirring. Thumping.

This human spirit I speak of, and which I aim to illuminate and illustrate, is inconvenient to the status quo. It's dangerous in the best possible way. And it's ready to participate in moral world creation if we'd just stop suffocating it in fear and obscuring it under exaggerated and psychologically inflated historical narratives.

There are, no doubt, many books on the shelves plainly pointing out that our world is in crisis. But it is not. It's in *revolt*. It's rebelling against itself. Not metaphorically, not physically, not economically, but *morally*. It is a world that desires to know its own history, even if that story is ugly and threatens to hollow out the forms of joy and blissful happiness which we are told are all around us. Because some of us are waking up to, or being accosted by, the unbearable cost of moral and spiritual compromise, and the absurd smallness of the extravagant rewards we've been offered in return.

The Evil Cognitive Dissonance Repairman

The true villain who lurks behind every argument laid out in this book is not a corrupt president, a tech billionaire, or a particular political party, though I have no love lost for any of them. It's a quieter figure who you will come to know quite well. I call him the *Cognitive Dissonance Repairman.*

He's your inner contractor, always on call. He fixes the cracks in your conscience before you even notice them. He has a whole toolbox full of philosophical glue, and psychological duct tape that tells you things like: "you're still a good person" (which you probably *are*), "you had no choice" (which might *really* be true), "this is just how the world works" (which is just an unimaginative rehash of the naturalistic fallacy), "this isn't even really happening" (which is a pretty unstable game), or "you actually are having a good *enough* time and everything is fine!" (which has been a surprisingly effective tool).

You didn't even hire this guy, but he always shows up for work. He's definitely not happy that you picked up this book, which is exactly why you should keep reading.

But let me make one thing clear. This is not a self-help book.

I don't really have anything against self-help books, and if you're helped by any of this, I doubt that either of us will complain. But I'm not here to help you "optimize your habits" or "unlock your potential." The book is not about you, at least not *specifically*. It's about us.

"Us," this strange embodied conscious creature with microwaves and mass graves, TikToks and testaments, slaves and saints, very good history books and a very bad History Channel. It's about the civilizational scaffolding we keep erecting and dismantling, about the moral plumbing under all our politics, and the curated histories we tell ourselves, and are told, to keep from having to rip it all out and start again.

The Cognitive Dissonance Repairman is not *just* an evil villain in this book. He's also a bit of a tragic figure. He means well, truly. He's been trying to protect you. But he's been doing it behind your back. And it's time we really question his motives.

This book is about confronting him, yes, but it's also about *negotiating* with him. Making peace, perhaps. Maybe even demanding that he check in with you before he gets to work. We're going to challenge some of his most powerful and beloved tools. I'm quite sure that you'll recognize them. You may already be using one right now, and we're only a few pages in.

To get the Repairman to sit at the negotiating table, we will have to tear down some of our most sacred moral narratives. We'll examine closely what we mean when we invoke the phrase "History will judge us" and I will urge us to retire it. History has no gavel. It's not a god. At best, it is a funhouse mirror. And we likely care far too much about how we look in the warped view. The vanity of our moral status to future generations is just as ugly as any of our current crimes.

The Prophets and Prophecies of Progress

Now, before the "progress pushers" begin to suspect that I am up to no good, before they clutch their charts and rush over to show me all of the ways in which the world has been undeniably improving and I should not be so harsh with "status quo thinking" and "the imperfect but generally net-gain global world order built upon neoliberalism" or *"enlightenment values,"* let me make another thing clear. This is *not* a book about progress denial. In fact, one of the most important arguments of this book is that we must *not* deny it. Too many books that take aim at the status quo, or rightly call out empire in its many forms, from colonialism to imperialism to economic neocolonialism, fall into a familiar trap. They downplay real aspects of progress and dismiss genuine gains. It might feel righteous to do so, but it distorts the picture, and misses the point.

I've sat on stages with Steven Pinker, one of the more prominent champions of the "things are getting better, relax with all this revolution talk" rhetoric, and I've obsessed over the interactive charts of Hans Rosling and others who insist we are living through an era of meaningful progress. And I'm not here to sneer. Much of their data *is* compelling. Though yes, the methodology behind it has been rightfully challenged by authors such as Rutger Bregman, Jason Hickel, and David Graeber, just to name a few. Hickel, in particular, offers a rather devastating rebuttal to Pinker's bogus data on the topic of abstract measures of extreme poverty in pre-colonized territories. There *are* many reasons to doubt the data, especially the cherry-picked "pre-history violence" stuff about the ancients and indigenous with their spears and skeletons, but that is not the focus of this book. I'll leave the data fights to others while I insist that the urge to hand-wave away the entire conceptual case is lazy and dishonest.

Something *like* progress happened. And it matters.

What this book offers is not a direct rebuttal to the Pinker-graphs, but a reframing of what it all means *morally*. I hope it becomes a companion conversation to consider what all that supposed progress has potentially cost, and, thus, why so much of it is now in danger or feels so utterly hollow.

"Burn It All Down?"

I'm never quite sure what people mean by this phrase.

I don't imagine that anything I write will spark a revolution that causes us to collectively forget the germ theory of disease, or how to build a rocket, or that women ought to have autonomy or the periodic table of elements. Don't worry, those helpful charts are safe. I don't think "burning it all down" means erasing hard-won truths like those, at least, I hope not.

In fact, some of what I argue might suggest that a certain kind of "burning it all down," philosophically speaking, could actually *expand* moral circles and unlock new forms of liberation. And if some of those so-called "regressive" revolutions turn out to be reactionary spasms born from unresolved moral frustration — the kind I'll be unpacking — then maybe we'll be slightly less afraid of the impulse to "burn it all down."

That said, yes, humans have, more than once, quite literally burned the world down. World wars, genocides, collapsed empires, we've seen what large-scale destruction looks like, and we know how quickly it can turn to ash. I'd like to think we'd all prefer to avoid that, or at least not be the ones twiddling our thumbs when the roof falls in.

So think of my argument not as a call to torch the world, but as an observational warning. The match is already lit, and the tinder is dry. If we have any chance of holding onto what's worth preserving *while* building something better, something designed not by default or inheritance, but by moral ambition and genuine human courage, then we need to radically rethink how we engage with history, how we conceive the moral opportunity of self-reflexive existence, and how we understand the purpose of moral philosophy.

History Beyond the Velvet Rope

To find this upgraded path, we'll be spending a great deal of time with "history" in these pages. Not to reenact moral victories or assign gold stars to modernity, but to ask deeper questions about what history is and what it's doing to us. We'll examine how the framing of history, as progress, as moral evidence, as verdict, has become one of the most powerful tools in the Cognitive Dissonance Repairman's toolkit. He loves history. The Repairman fashions himself as quite the historian, in fact. He has turned history itself into a morality play where we are always the enlightened ones. But this book is going to press pause on that auto-narration.

Much of this book will place us in what feels like an eternal existential predicament. The tension between "history" and "morality" is not new. It has not changed, and it likely never will.

But we *are* also living through something that is genuinely new. Access to history has been flung wide open. You no longer need a university library or an academic credential to wander the back corridors of the past. Many of us have access to ChatGPT, Wikipedia, open archives, and machine-learning tour guides scattered across the Internet, ready to answer our late-night questions about colonial tax codes, the Peloponnesian War, the original illustrator of the Smokey Bear logo, or the exchange rate of gold to the Uzbekistan sum graphed over time. Whatever your bouncy brain wants, it is there, packaged and delivered in a linguistic style of your choosing.

It is exhilarating. It is destabilizing. And it is threatening, especially to those who once held the keys to the museum and preferred that you stay behind the velvet rope.

The very idea of historical "expertise" is under fascinating stress at the time of my writing. This is making a lot of people very nervous. The Repairman isn't thrilled about this development either. Perfect.

Suddenly, you can go snooping around in the timelines he'd rather curate for you to ensure that you aren't disillusioned with the shopping malls and capitalism. And while all this historical back-room access doesn't *guarantee* better thinking, it *does* make this a particularly ripe moment to ask what, exactly, we're doing when we call something "history" and questioning if we are really "better moral people" than those frozen in the museum display cases.

This exploration will surface the understudied difference between building "better worlds" and cultivating "better people." I'll be interrogating the role of the historian, not just as a chronicler of facts, but as a cultural architect with surprising influence over how we justify the present. We'll ask what it means to say a society has *improved*. Who gets to say it? And why we feel such a strong need for the past to bless us and the future to thank us.

This is not just a book *about* history, it's a book that wants to destabilize the way we lean on history, especially when it has been advertised as a kind of moral laundering service for the unjust status quo.

Opportunity over Obligation

This book is also a proposal. I'm inviting you to reframe morality not as a burden of divine or natural *obligation,* nor as a vapid iteration of choosing lesser evils, but as a series of human *opportunities*. Opportunities to live with integrity. To notice what matters. To resist despair. This is not about moral sainthood. This is about ending the process of moral atrophy and moral delegation. It's about building up the muscle of *moral readiness,* the capacity to feel a moment of painful clarity when it arrives and not flinch. To act not because you *must,* but because you *can*. And to notice when you truly *can't*. And in those moments when there really is "no choice" to not shrug. To not change the subject. To not pretend everything is okay. Everything, it turns out, is *not* okay when we "don't have a choice."

You will come to know the gravitational center of my entire moral philosophy and existential orientation is defined by the insistence of a simple phrase: *Opportunity Over Obligation*. After spending time studying the tendency to paraphrase and compress entire eras, philosophers, authors, wars, labor struggles, and time periods down to very concise single lines or phrases which might end up on museum plaques or in biographical blurbs, I would not object to being vaguely remembered in some pretentious future cocktail party like this, "Jay Shapiro? Oh yeah, it kind of rings a bell. Wasn't he that very handsome author who stressed Opportunity Over Obligation?" (Feel free to omit the aesthetic adjective if you must, but make sure you get the last part right.)

I aim to show you how this seemingly innocent shift in existential and moral orientation is a big deal, and how it's likely much more difficult, more profound, and more precarious than it strikes you here in the introduction.

Discomfort Ahead

I've stressed that this is a dangerous book for the status quo. And I mean that not just in social, global, or political senses, I mean it in the personal sense. It really might knock you off a comfortable perch, if you happen to be lucky enough (or blissfully ignorant enough) to be feeling that kind of thing these days. But if we are honest with ourselves, we know that the status quo, and the totality of its future promises, is a catastrophically insufficient reward for the price of your moral integrity.

If you feel that in your bones — if you've ever had a moment, even a flicker, where something didn't sit right, whether that be that a newsflash of a distant atrocity, a homeless man and dog asking you for coins outside an overpriced coffee shop, or noticing an unsavory alliance of the company that signs your paycheck, and the Repairman whispered you back to moral slumber, then I hope you'll read on. Because in that fleeting, nearly imperceptible, blink, there is a small but important moral fissure. Before it gets patched up, let's pry it open and take a look.

I recall a particular fissure-filled summer that has, over time, solidified into something like my personal philosophical origin myth, a hinge after which certain questions would never leave me and certain feelings would not be un-felt. It didn't start as a grand revelation, but it planted the seeds of unease and wonder that have grown, unruly and persistent, into the book you're holding now and my desire to understand how the moral threads of history, ideology, technology, and the political economy intertwine.

This is how I remember it.

The Pringles Can at the Edge of Empire: A Brief History of How I Became a Problem

The summer I was supposed to go to Israel, I ended up in a slum in Ghana. This destination was largely accidental. Or maybe it was something closer to fate, if fate sometimes wears the disguise of teenage rebellion and geographic logistics.

In the Conservative Jewish community where I was raised in Allentown, Pennsylvania, the Israel trip wasn't just a rite of passage, it was the *real* Bar Mitzvah, the one that was supposed to happen a few years after the pimple punctuated Torah portion and awkward cousins-meeting-friends-on-a-dance-floor party. The Israel summer trip functionally served as the final chapter once you'd graduated from the Holocaust-heavy curriculum that passed for Jewish education.

Everyone in my Jewish circle was going. The kitchen tables and mailboxes were stuffed with glossy brochures showing sunburnt, metal-mouthed teens draped across one another's shoulders, grinning atop hilltops, gazing out over stoney desert landscapes with their arms slung like they'd just conquered something. The touring companies with names carefully pulled from Hebrew texts to convey just the right amount of solemn promises and exotic adventures had logos of defiant lions, elaborate candelabras, and bold stars emblazoned in gold and silver and blue and white. They vied for the winning paper position, flipping upward in the race to collect the signed check and curate your son's "transformative summer."

The itineraries were tight, and tightly controlled. Culture, beaches, Bible stories. The included locations (and not-so-subtly omitted ones) were all observed and "protected" by the occasional sunglassed straight jawed soldier who seemed to come from the same mold used for the G.I. Joe action figures stuffed away in some soon to be forgotten childhood toy box. Time to put pretend away and encounter the actual dangers. You were about to become a man.

It all looked fun enough, I suppose. But something in me revolted. Maybe it was ideological. Maybe it was instinctual. Maybe it was just classic teenage contrarianism, which I had been perfecting for a few years on all fronts. I had been exposed, ever so slightly, to the political truths lurking under the brochures by the late night MTV News updates that showed young Palestinian boys tossing rocks and catching the occasional live round in their necks. I didn't fully understand it, but it was clear that I was discouraged from doing precisely that. I didn't like being told what I could and could not understand.

So, whatever it was, I sat my parents down and made a counteroffer. What if, instead of Israel, I used the money they'd set aside to go somewhere else entirely? Somewhere I didn't already have a script for. Somewhere unfamiliar, unbranded. I mean, I could *always* do the Israel thing later. Don't they have those free trips for people like me? It's just good, solid rational economics, right?

My pitch wasn't exactly a threat, but it also wasn't a request. I was not going to be a happy camper on the standard propaganda tour. My older brother had been shuffled off on one of these tours three years earlier and had come home with the unironic gift of a green and gold IDF T-shirt, a souvenir I wore to Junior High a few times out of, let's just say the word, *obligation*.

I was thirteen when that shirt was handed to me.

By sixteen, sitting at that table with my parents, I'd learned a thing or two about the "conflict" and the shirt was very neatly folded at the bottom of an otherwise messy teenage drawer. To their credit, or perhaps in a moment of parental fatigue and defeat, they agreed to my plan/threat. A few days later, my mother brought home a brochure from an organization that ran summer trips for high schoolers to a plethora of global locations. It was a blend of homestay, community service, adventure, and just enough risk to make you feel worldly. I flipped through the options and circled two places I knew almost nothing about: Thailand and Ghana. Ghana ended up winning out because the group flew out of JFK, not LAX, and my dad wanted to drive me to the airport and save a few thousand miles of gas.

And that's how I found myself, at sixteen-going-on-seventeen, walking through the red-dusted edge of Accra, surrounded by unfamiliar smells, crumbling buildings, barefoot children with impossibly big smiles seeking my address, and the hum of something morally bothersome I couldn't yet name. The year was 1999.

I remember the sweat, the sun, the weight of not knowing what to do with my hands during endless stilted greetings. Was it right or left? I remember watching a boy carry water on his head while laughing so hard he nearly toppled over. Before the trip, I think my entire knowledge of Africa consisted of what I saw in *The Lion King*, the Sally Struthers Save-The-Children-Foundation tele campaigns on late night cable, and from the leafed-through pages of *National Geographic* magazines I found in waiting rooms. Dancing lions and the circle of life, famine-stricken children with swollen bellies and flies on their faces, or photos of bare-chested old women with their insane looking facial piercings. But now that I was there, what I was seeing, feeling, hearing was *none* and *all* of that mashed together. I remember the gut-level realization. I didn't know *anything* about the world. But I was suddenly, unmistakably inside it.

It was a hot cascading avalanche of thoughts. Thoughts I wasn't equipped to process. I knew, in the abstract, that poverty existed. But I had never been in direct contact with so much of it. Of course, I also knew the slave trade and European colonialism had happened, and I knew it was one of history's deepest moral wounds. I'd seen Alex Haley's *Roots*. I could invoke the light sprinklings of history to *try* to make sense of this intense environment which was screaming out for explanation. But it wasn't making much moral sense.

I thought of all my Jewish friends who *had* chosen one of the glossy "arms over Masada" brochures. They were likely facing very little challenge explaining what they were encountering at the Western Wall or floating in some salty sea. In fact, no one in that community was likely to even ask about their experience. Everyone had that story committed to memory. They were probably having "fun." But I was not envious at all. This is what I wanted.

Throughout the days of contact with this very foreign form of poverty, I also knew my family had a washing machine and dinner on the table back home in Pennsylvania. I knew, again, abstractly, that my life was coddled and privileged and that was not everyone's reality. But that contrast had never pressed against me in three dimensions.

I was having trouble even keeping up with my bad adolescent diary entries. My go-to mix of melancholy poetry and borrowed Counting Crows lyrics to share with the other teens on the trip was not even worth trying. Well, I *did* try those things, but even my teenage self knew it was performative autopilot dribble that the Grad-School aged trip leaders politely endured during evening circle gatherings. I was simply paralyzed by the scale of what I didn't understand.

One early morning, while staying in a small village named Imano Praso, about two hours inland from Cape Coast, where our little group was helping build a pavilion for a primary school, I took a walk alone. The village was small enough that our group of twelve American teens snapping disposable photos and giggling about the strange food was an ongoing local event. A week earlier, they had welcomed us, awkwardly and beautifully, in a ceremony that felt both generous and undeserved. I had probably seen every face that lived there, all gathered around one of my forever-embarrassed trip-mates who they had hilariously and sincerely draped in Kente cloth and to whom they presented a wooden drum. I snapped a few photos of that ceremony which froze some of their curious dark eyes onto film that I would get developed back home at the sterile suburban elevator music CVS pharmacy. Those Kodak eyes have yet to stop asking me what I was doing there.

Over the weeks, I had become increasingly aware that I carried a romantic notion, however poorly formed, about what I was hoping to spiritually "discover" in Africa. That maybe here, in the "non-West," in the colonized side of the world, in the oppressed shadow of empire, far from the stale, predictable, comforts of minivans and climate control, I would find a kind of forgotten ancient wisdom. A life more connected to nature. More grounded. More *real*. Maybe the lack of well paved roads and Nintendo systems came with a hidden compensation. Wholeness? Fulfillment? Natural rhythm? I *wanted* that to be true. I *wanted* these people to be enlightened and have the keys to happiness and impart lessons about contentment's unrelatedness to material wealth. How condescending of me.

That habit of romanticizing and fetishizing the Global South is one I now see more clearly. It flatters no one, and harms both romanticized and romanticizer alike. But at the time, as I moved my new sneakers along the sunbaked dirt path, I was guilty of it, still desperately trying to make the math work in my head. Suffering minus luxury equals enlightenment? Maybe the story would be that I didn't go to Israel to float in a morally fraught propagandized religious mythology about a divine chosen family and ancestral belonging, but I went to Africa and discovered the *true* human touchstones of contentment and peace in what "the West" foolishly pities and sends aid to. It sounded like the kind of story an angsty rebellious teenager might like. But it wasn't hanging together in my mind.

As a documentary filmmaker, I've since had the interesting experience, many times, of strolling through deeply poverty-stricken African ghettos with Westerners who are seeing it for the first time. It's uncanny how often people say to themselves, and each other, upon exiting the ghetto and catching their breath, "Well, they're poor but they're happy." This is a load of garbage. But I think there is something very interesting in the hunch to say it which relates to the title of this book.

But on that mild morning while the light was pink and soft and the sun rose over green forested slopes, I thought that the nature part of the experience, whatever I would remember it to be, was simply beautiful and mercifully uncontroversial. I paused to admire it. I looked out at the drifting stream, tracing the landscape. There were colorful birds fluttering with exotic songs I didn't know against leaf shapes I was still learning. Maybe, *this* was the peace that I could touch? Maybe this vision of an unpopulated, pre-man natural state is something more readily available and crucial to remember? Was *that* the lesson of this trip? And just as the intellectual ping-pong in my mind began to subside, I saw her.

An older woman from the village, whom I immediately recognized to be one of the many smiling dancers from the welcome ceremony, was bent over in the water. She was no longer posing for a photo-op destined for a 16-year-old's plastic "Summer of '99" photo album. She was out there doing what she does during a regular morning in this patch of Earth. She was washing T-shirts by hand, crooked like a bent paperclip and bare-chested, scrubbing hard with defined triceps which bulged with a suddenly complicated political signal about her age, income, and labor. I imagined mosquitos bursting from tiny egg clumps, glued to the undersides of sharp reeds. They helicoptered up and hissed near her weary eardrums. If I'd tried to ignore them, and the too-defined muscles, I could have attempted to describe the scene as poetic, spiritual, grounding, something that echoed my *National Geographic* preconception. But what I actually thought at that moment was this: *She could really use a damn washing machine.* And I didn't know what to do with that thought.

Did it make me a capitalist stooge? A Western apologist? Was it honest? Was it wrong? I didn't know. I didn't even know how to answer the questions of why she *didn't* have one. So, I looked away and continued toward the half-built school, telling myself I was here to help.

A week later, while on the homestay part of the summer, I was walking alone again, this time in the crowded, chaotic city of Kumasi, where motorbikes growl, chickens flap and fight, and blown out radio speakers blare DJs who seem to always yell stuff while the music plays. Vendors shout over one another, all hawking the same things for the same prices. I was thinking again about the woman in the stream and *my* washing machine which diligently waited for me back home, along with the reliable city plumbing system which functioned on magic for all I knew. I was trying to prepare myself for how I'd explain the moment when I got back home. Maybe I *would* defend the West, I thought. Maybe modernity wasn't so bad. Maybe all this chaos I was seeing out here in Ghana was just some necessary stage of "development" that was generally trending in the "right" direction. And maybe they just have to get through these stages of "corruption" and distrust. Maybe it is a moral action to make this place look a little more like Allentown and "we" should be bringing it there unapologetically. And then I turned a corner and looked where the cluttered stacked buildings parted, opening to a busy intersection, and I saw a massive twenty-foot-tall cylinder, built smack in the middle of the roundabout. It was an advertisement, a giant concrete replica of a Pringles can. Bright red, gleaming, absurd. The smiling mustachioed mascot beamed like a cartoon god over the slum. The promise of progress had planted a beacon, and it was salty.

I had a lot of questions.

Cracks were forming in my worldview. And over the many decades since that surreal Pringles monument and that woman in the stream, those cracks have widened into full-blown canyons. I've studied philosophy, made documentary films about international law and sports, argued my way out of moral labyrinths and back into them, and found myself reluctantly conscripted into one fraught global conversation after another with popular intellectuals garnering huge platforms. September

11th, Iraq, Palestine, climate collapse, AI, neoliberalism, take your pick.

I've changed my mind more than once. Been humbled, outmaneuvered by my own weakness, re-convinced, started over. I've learned to challenge my instincts and refine my arguments, and I've tried — *really tried* — to remain open without becoming hollow. And yet, through all of it, I keep returning to that woman in the stream and that grinning Pringles can, planted like a joke at the edge of empire.

I still want to make sense of it. I still want to answer his smiling challenge with something insightful and powerful. And I think, maybe, I finally can.

The Pressure of History

I know that trip changed me. Not in the tidy, résumé-ready way you write about in college essays (though I *did*, of course, write about it in my very cliche one). But in the way a crack changes the structural integrity of a wall. I didn't have the words for it back then, not in Ghana, not even years later in college. But what was haunting me in that moment wasn't just poverty or injustice or the absurdity of capitalism. It was something deeper. I was starting to feel the pressure of history, its weight, its silence, its crooked judgment. And I had no idea where I stood inside it.

This is a book about morality and rethinking moral progress, yes, but it's also a book about what we do, and what we *ought* to do, with the past. And I will, at times, be pointing this probing question at myself. I don't intend to lecture from some plinth of psychological exclusion.

Whether or not *morality itself* exists in some perfect, objective timeless vacuum is a question I'll tackle, or be tackled by, in the deepest existential chapters. But what's certain, once we learn to pay attention, is that *moral decisions* don't happen in a vacuum. They happen in time. In context. They happen in a mess of memory and power and lust and narratives of shame and love and fear. And somewhere between the idea of *eternal moral truths* and the *realities of the present moment,* a whole waterfall of anxiety and art and moral improvisation crashes through. Lucky us.

So, before we start talking about how to live engaged lives of moral bravery in an eternal contest with our powerful shapeshifting evil Cognitive Dissonance Repairmen, we need to ask the first question which sparks Chapter 1: **What the heck is "history" and how does morality relate to it?**

Chapter 1

Judging History

Flipping the tables on who gets to make the verdict

A Very Brave Announcement

I've decided to boycott the transatlantic slave trade.

I find chattel slavery morally reprehensible, and I will no longer contribute to its demand. So, from now on, I will refuse to purchase any goods produced by the hands of African captives forced onto ships and sold into brutal agricultural labor across the Americas. I'll be taking this boycott seriously, especially at grocery stores and clothing outlets. I encourage you to join me.

Now, before you check the copyright date on this book to make sure it hasn't been miscategorized by a confused shopkeeper, I will confess that I'm writing this in the early 21st century. If you sense that the timing of my proclamation slightly dilutes the moral heroism of the boycott, congratulations, you're thinking clearly and you are sensing that "moral decisions" and "history" have an intertwined relationship.

Still, it's worth noting that slavery (of the specific historical type I am describing) was, and remains, a moral abomination. And the fact that you and I can recognize that across centuries, cultures, and continents might tell us something important about moral truths. But the act of *responding* to those truths, of making decisions in their light, is a wildly messy, contextual, time-bound affair.

I am not suggesting that slavery was ever *not* immoral, nor that a boycott would ever be anything less than moral. But I think it is easy to notice that boycotting the transatlantic slave trade *today* isn't any kind of moral triumph. It's easy. It costs me nothing. It's a souvenir from a war long over, a stance no longer requiring any real courage. It wasn't always like this. Some people took that stand when it was dangerous, costly, and wildly unpopular. Plenty, probably most, didn't.

Does that mean that absent any kind of personal "risk" or "sacrifice" there can be no moral choices?

That question presents us with a quietly explosive truth. Moral positions *might* be timeless, but moral action *never* is.

It happens in confusion, in compromise, under pressure, in silence, and in eerily banal stillness engineered by the Cognitive Dissonance Repairman (the lurking villain we will meet in Chapter 3).

Moral action happens when the moral outcome isn't yet "historically obvious." When the "right side of history" hasn't been printed on T-shirts or codified in history books. But before we talk about how to better comprehend and encounter that unclaimed moral ground, we need to spend this chapter thinking deeply about the medium in which moral action is embedded. That medium's name is ***history***.

History as Emergent Waves of Bullets and Love Letters

Sometimes we picture history as a timeline. A clean progression of facts, neatly arranged. Event follows event, cause follows effect, all strung together by the mysterious arrow of time, one thing after another until —voilà —the present. But a timeline is a lie. Or at least, a wild oversimplification. It is a line which, perhaps arbitrarily, connects the dots between things which happened into a shape we might refer to as "history." But this is not philosophically rich. We can do much better than that.

A better analogy is considering history to be an *emergent* phenomenon. Like an ocean wave, which is formed by millions of tiny events and actions, none of which "know" they are constituting anything bigger. This image, the wave, is one that I find useful, even if, as I'll soon argue, it *too* falls well short of elucidating that elusive thing called "history." But let's try it on for size first. I find that it fits in an all-too-comforting way.

Picture a vast ocean. Crests, swells, and ripples extend to the horizon. Some patches are turbulent with foam, others are dull and still. Now, focus on one wave. Zoom close to it. Closer still, down to the water's surface. Crash in until the blue fills your frame. Closer again within that water, until you're looking at just a single molecule. Two parts hydrogen, one part oxygen.

That molecule in front of you, spinning and vibrating, has no idea it's part of a wave, let alone an ocean. If we zoom in even further, down to the level of quantum weirdness, we lose even the shape and idea of the molecule or atoms themselves. Hazy notions like superposition, entanglement, and non-locality start to blur the edges of reality. (Don't worry, this book is not attempting a grand unifying theory of physics. I'll settle for a unifying theory of political, moral, and existential analysis.) At the quantum and even the molecule scales, there's no "ocean wave" to be seen. Just apparent vaguely watery chaos.

Now, zoom back out, slowly, and something starts to emerge. Molecule after wiggling molecule, randomness starts to look patterned, the offset wobbles begin to look coordinated. The surface of the water soon shimmers and rolls. Pull back further and the wave itself becomes visible again. Pull back even more, and we see the tide. That's emergence. Contingent macro patterns form from the action of the none-the-wiser constituent micro parts. And it's one way, not the best way, but an illuminating way, to think about history.

The Iron Age. The Iran-Contra Affair. The Fall of Rome. The Enlightenment. The Cold War. The Russian Revolution. The Grunge Music Movement in Seattle. Your Grandparents' Wedding Night. These are history-wave names. But inside those waves, the real stuff, the micro chaos churned. And much of it is yet to even be imagined or remembered.

So, for a demonstration, let's zoom into a particular violently sloshing history-wave with the name "The Civil War." We can see it crashing on the surface. Let's plunge.

As we travel closer towards it, we see some other patterns in watery shapes. The "breakdown of The Missouri Compromise from 1820" just flashed at us along with the Kansas-Nebraska

Act in 1854 which, from this still somewhat zoomed out level, tells an obvious story of "deepening cultural divides and economic tensions which played out over decades."

We get closer, splashing through the water surface, and the Secession Crisis of 1860 slides into view. Diving deeper and closer, you see 11 states agreeing to form the Confederacy and casting votes in wig-filled humid capital buildings. Turbulent water is all around us now and we're losing sight of the entire wave. The Emancipation Proclamation just zipped by. We can see dueling newspaper headlines. A man purchases a fresh *Chicago Tribune,* dated January 3rd, 1863. The text displays "The Great Proclamation." Another man picks up the *Richmond Daily Dispatch* two days later with the words "an incitement to insurrection." He leafs to the classified ads offering a fifty-dollar reward for the return or imprisonment of a "stout healthy negro man named Jim who ran away on Christmas Day near Hanover Junction." Let's plunge further down to the molecule level, barely remembering that we are somewhere in the "Civil War Wave."

We're now at the level where molecules slosh and wiggle around in a barely cohesive way. From here, we can see the Siege of Vicksburg in 1863 and a narrative of "a critical Union victory at the Mississippi River splitting the Confederacy in two."

Let's plunge deep towards just a few isolated molecules.

We fly by a scene in Lancaster, Ohio that catches our eye. A baby is cradled in the arms of Charles Sherman in 1820 as he grants his newborn son the middle name "Tecumseh" in honor of the fallen Shawnee leader and warrior. Mister Sherman does not know that this little baby will go on to lead an infamous and devastating march some 44 years later, nor that he will later advocate for the extermination and forced removal of Native Americans for the expansion of railroads and settlements, the very forces which his "Indian" namesake resisted during his lifetime. We can almost see faces and hear human cries at this close scale.

I know you are tempted to stay with this story and trace these tantalizing molecules through the wave. I've provided some enticing details. Pay attention to that feeling. Notice how you have a strong desire to "know the narrative," to ask, "what happened next?" Don't worry, I won't leave you frustrated forever. I'll be revisiting Tecumseh later, but more importantly, I'll be dissecting our insatiable lust for moral narrative.

Now, let's make one last zoomed in plunge elsewhere, even closer, to a tiny patch of quantum stuff where cannons and muskets are blasting gun smoke into thick hot air. One last breath before the very closest zoom we'll make.

And here we are. Splash.

~~~

Calloused fingerprint ridges tremble on cold dark metal.

It's June of 1862 in a town called Port Republic, Virginia. A battle is underway. There are about 1600 troops wearing blue. They gather with their musket sights set on a bridge flanked with red-cotton-clad gunmen.

Get a good look at the individual soldier whose finger looms large. Do you see the sweat forming on his lip in this swampy humidity? Do you hear his thumping heartbeat rattle the thread-loose metal button by his breast pocket? Look *inside* that breast pocket and see the ink-bled letter from Susan, his young pregnant bride who at that very moment is plucking a ragweed from the family plot in Georgia and thinking of our soldier whose name we have learned from her kissed salutation is "Samuel, my beloved." Turn your attention back to Samuel's ash darkened finger as it tightens around the trigger. Stay here at this scale, just this finger on metal.
~~~

In our physics analogy of an emergent ocean wave, we zeroed in, as much as our theories, imaginations, and knowledge currently allow, on an atomized physical description of something which exists in a larger physical description. We can think of those "physical wave things" as existing in a concept of "space." The wave takes up a certain amount of space, as do the tiny molecules within it. But when we shift this practice of deconstructing emergence to the ideas of "history," we are now trying to zero in on *time* rather than space, which is much trickier.

So, this *moment*, this tiny sliver of activity as Samuel grits his teeth and squeezes the trigger, is a micro constituent instance of what amounted to "America's Civil War" as named by historians, politicians, poets, the winners, and the survivors. And just like a single wiggling oxygen molecule in an ocean wave, whether Samuel's just-fired bullet plunges between Union rib bones and tears into the heart of another man in another bloody uniform who also has a sweat-stained letter in his pocket; or if the bullet misses all of its human targets only to lodge itself in the knotted roots of a young oak tree which was minding its own damn business before the humans showed up with guns, it's of no great significance to the totality of the historical fact of the "American Civil War." Though, to Susan and her descendants, it was surely a crucial fact, as it was, of course, to the geological "history" of that poor oak tree who may not have minded the human flesh interception.

But just as this personally monumental and historically inconsequential bullet explodes out of the barrel, let's quickly pull ourselves away from this molecule way back out to the view of the whole wave of The Civil War. We know that this is not the furthest view one can take. A single ocean wave is merely an event of what amounts to something even larger, the "tide." And the "tide" can be taken as an event in a "season," or an "epoch," or a "climate trend." The scale and scope of our vantage point couches events and phenomena like nesting dolls of emergence which ultimately maxes out at something like "the entire universal history" at the biggest doll and a "quanta of a singular contextless sensation" at the smallest.

"History," it turns out, is a very strange nesting doll to locate.

So, Samuel's bullet hit or missed. Either way, the ocean kept rolling. And unless there were millions of bullets that were all hitting or missing with some kind of common intention, the wave didn't bother to notice, and we don't need to think about it very much to predict and define the history-wave itself.

That's emergence. And that is an analogy for history which I will use throughout this book, even while letting you know that I *know* it is a false analogy with many problems.

Some Problems with the Wave

History as a wave has its poetic appeal. But it also comes at a cost. Because people are not water molecules.

Samuel's sweat, Susan's prayer, the ragweed in her hand, they're real. Their choices and sensations matter in a way that the wave imagery can't quite capture. History isn't just water moving according to some indifferent tide. It's people struggling, hesitating, guessing, betting their lives on stories they can barely see beyond.

The wave analogy also misses the mark as it seems to suggest that history is something you simply measure or uncover, like a buried fossil or a perfectly preserved time capsule just waiting to be unearthed, unchanged, and decoded. That it moves forward with force and inevitability, indifferent to the internal drama of its human components. But that's not how it works. History is not just a bunch of facts which "speaks for itself." It doesn't simply roll forward and reveal itself to the diligent excavator. It has to be told, stitched together, shaped. It has to be narrated.

It needs an interpreter.

And depending on who's doing the stitching, and what moral outcome they want the story to explain, the same facts can take wildly different forms. This is not a flaw in historical thinking. It's its nature. And it brings us to another problem with the wave. It hides the narrator. It hides the fact that the process of "history-making" is morally laden from the start. So, before we can confront history's role as a moral compass (or a moral weapon), we need to get clear on something foundational: **facts don't speak. People do.**

The Double Life of History

The words "history" and "histories" don't lend themselves to meaningful definition absent the thread of moral theory. But if I were forced to offer you a scientific definition — something cold, tidy, and academically passable — it might go like this:

> *History is a theory of causal relationships between a string of past events presented as a cohesive explanatory narrative. And, like any good explanation, it should contain some predictive and prescriptive knowledge. Therefore, histories are narratives which cast the relations of instances, events, and beliefs into a story which sufficiently explains an outcome — often, that outcome is what we call the "present."*

It's not a terrible definition. It holds together. But even in its restraint, it seems to aspire to something that history has never quite been and will never be able to be: an objective science. A cool, analytical method of ordering what has happened without providing subtle suggestions of what *ought* to have happened. It strives to be a dispassionate system of cause and effect. But "history" resists this. Because the raw material of history — people, memory, belief, conflict, interpretation — is anything but neutral, and it simply isn't how we humans package and remember information. We seek explanation through storytelling and moral fable.

We rarely use the word "history" in isolation. It's nearly always accompanied by a qualifier to define what *type* of history we're talking about, or, more precisely, what *outcome* we want to explain.

Is it a "family history," a "national history," a "history of a person, a thing, a place, or institution," a "geological history of a specific rainforest"? Once we identify *what* we're trying to explain, we begin to look backward for events that support that explanation. If something contributes to that explanatory chain, we say it "makes the history books." That's a lovely bit of linguistic evidence. Even the coldest framing of history as an objective scientific method ends in a poetic narrative gesture towards literature. And that's the deeper point. Even when we dress it up in objectivity, history never escapes its narrative roots. And the etymology of the word itself betrays that entanglement.

The word ἱστορία (*historia*) first appears in Greek in the 5th century BCE. It was used by Herodotus to describe his systematic investigation of past events. Back then, "history" meant "inquiry," "investigation," or "learning through inquiry."

A few centuries later, Romans like Cicero and Livy borrowed the term and incorporated it into Latin, where its meaning subtly shifted toward "an account" or "narrative." By the time the word arrived in Old French in the 9th century as *estoire,* it had fully taken on both meanings — story and inquiry — and was used in medieval chronicles and romances that often blurred the line between fact and fiction. Books like *The History of the English People* by Geoffrey Gaimar in 1136 wove real events together with legends like King Arthur's round table.

By the Renaissance, "history" began to circle back to its Greek roots and reemphasize "a scholarly inquiry into the past." And yet, the narrative element never went away. It couldn't. Because there is no such thing as history without storytelling.

I doubt we've settled, even now, on what kind of thing history truly is. It continues to twist between the poles of story and science, forever unsettled, forever reshaping itself depending on who's doing the telling and why.

For the remainder of this book — and hopefully for the remainder of your thinking days — you should be aware of how the existentially tortured duality of the word "history" echoes the deeper tension of the human condition itself. We are creatures stitched between ***science*** and ***story***, between logic and longing, between the "manifest view of man" and the "scientific view of man" as the philosopher Wilfrid Sellars explained in his 1962 essay *Philosophy and the Scientific Image of Man*. In it, Sellars beautifully lays out how neither view (the objective theoretical mathematically describable view and the apparent, experiential, and emotional view) are complete alone, and it is philosophy's task to somehow fuse these two images in a coherent, unified picture of humanity. I tend to read this tension as a brilliant framing of the famous mind-body problem which surfaces again and again in philosophy when we contend with undeniable brute fact of consciousness and its mysterious relationship with what appears to be the non-conscious physical world.

This entanglement, between story and science, is not just a quirk of the word "history." It's a mirror of how we experience the world. It reflects the deep human tendency to both seek truth and shape it, to explain and to mythologize, often in the same breath, all in the tortured service of seeking moral belonging in a universe not of our creation. This entangled structure is both generative and destabilizing, and I will return to it in more depth. But for now, let's keep both shadows of the word in view as we move toward the next trouble spot.

Empire Flags and Memory Shrinkage

At the time of this writing, the violence between Ukraine and Russia does not yet have much of a global consensus name. Ukrainian outlets, and its allies, tend to refer to it as the "Russian-Ukrainian War" (always listing Russia first) while Russian outlets refer to it as a "special military operation," and have even instituted penalties for outlets who use the morally loaded "w" word to describe it. I doubt that either side will achieve such a total victory in the near term as to completely seize the naming trophy.

The difficulty with being doomed to "live through the medium of history" is that we are trapped at a super zoomed in level of the sloshing and wiggling waters that we know are part of larger waves with shapes, directions, and causal relations that we can't quite comprehend. If only we could somehow zoom out and away, into the future, and inspect our situation from afar, to see our molecule selves in context.

Will a future historian write about battles in Vuhledar, Ukraine in a similar way to the battle at Port Republic, Virginia, in which my fictional Samuel fought? Will that historian couch the destruction of the Antonovka Road Bridge in the context of a much larger struggle? Will it make sense to include certain battles in their history books only if the outcome is a clear military victory for one side? Or is the entire outbreak of violence over the past few years going to be compressed into a single flareup in a more zoomed out historical narrative about "Violent Resistance to NATO Expansion" or "The Fanatical Fantasies of Deluded Soviet Nostalgia" or even something resource-leaning like "The Uranium Field Wars"? (Ukraine holds significant uranium reserves, which could be crucial for both energy production and military applications, depending on the alliance or "sphere of influence" it aligns with.)

You must have noticed how I smuggled in two very different morally laden possible nametags for all this violence. But aside from the moral framing in question, we should first appreciate the possibility that a war like this which fills up our news cycles might not be included in future history books very often, if at all.

If you doubt that entire wars might be reduced to single, barely mentioned, nodes of much larger historical campaigns, just think of how we might now pick up a history book and read about "The Reconquista" which spanned entire centuries (8th through 15th). This seven-century-long "event" was comprised of many groupings of wars with names like "Astur-Leonese Wars," "The Toledo Campaigns," "The Almoravid Wars," and "The Almohad Wars," just to name a few. Did the people living and dying through those centuries know that they were participating in something that would be compressed into just two words? I highly doubt it.

To really drive the point home, imagine you're 25 years old in the year 1492, the generally accepted end of *The Reconquista*. That means roughly 31 generations of your family had come and gone since the year this history-wave began, way back in 718. We're not talking about your parents, your grandparents, or even your great-grandparents. The sentence would have to be something like, "Oh yeah, my great-great-great-great" (say it 29 times) "grandfather was around when that all kicked off."

I don't even know the names of my great-grandparents, and I couldn't tell you anything about my great(x29)th-grandfather.

"But that is an *old* wave," you might say. Older waves tend to only be known and spoken about from those zoomed out levels because our knowledge is scarcer. "The Reconquista" ended 600 years ago and has a more distant cause-effect relationship on our present than something in our century. The compression and reduction in our teaching and learning about those old waves makes sense.

True enough. But even more recent waves such as "The Korean War" or the "Soviet Invasion of Afghanistan" are already both being slotted by historians into the same larger narrative of "The Cold War." I would guess that less-than-31-future-generations-from-now high school students might one day hear about "The Cold War" in a passing paragraph and only discover the individual wars named after places that might no longer exist like the "Korean War"* or "Vietnam War" if they decide to pursue a doctorate in a particularly esoteric era of History (or ask their chatbot for "deep research").

That might sound crazy or depressing, or both.

**Note that I am using the current American naming convention for this conflict. I happen to be an American-born author and will likely default towards an American linguistic bias throughout this book. I will try, and surely fail, to announce my awareness of this crutch. In later chapters, I will contend with the moral complications of such semantic indoctrination and cultural myopia. For example, in South Korea, the same violence I am referring to is known as Yook-i-o Jeonjaeng which translates to "The 6/25 War," simply named for the war's start date on June 25, 1950. In North Korea, it is known as Joguk Haebang Jeonjaeng or "The Fatherland Liberation War." In China, it's called Kàngměi Yuáncháo Zhànzhēng or "The War to Resist U.S. Aggression and Aid Korea." In China and South Korea, the term "Cold War" is generally accepted, and this violence is slotted into that larger narrative. In North Korea, "Cold War" is rarely used, and it would be more common to place the conflict in a narrative about resistance to imperialism and the North Korean philosophy of self-reliance (Juche), though it is understood to be part of the broader United States led opposition to communism. So, with apologies and to not paralyze our discussion, I will continue on with acknowledgment that the linguistic framings I am using are unavoidably compromised.*

The Korean War is estimated to have claimed the lives of up to 1.5 million civilians and 900,000 soldiers. How could something so devastatingly big and life altering for those who suffered through it be reduced to one of a series of footnote battles in what amounts to a larger historical narrative about what is likely to be a story about two short-lived hegemonic nations trapped in an "influence and resource" rivalry?

Can you not imagine a human just a few centuries from now strolling through a museum and coming across a display that reads, "The Cold War of the 20th Century," which lists "The Korean War," "The Vietnam War," "Arab-Israeli Conflicts," "The Cambodian War," "The Ethiopian Civil War," and others in fine print italics at the bottom of the display, apparently best understood as mere variables in a larger equation about global cultural dominance? Perhaps this museumgoer will think the whole thing is strange, this bitter rivalry with such deeply inflamed passions between two, now defunct, empires with funny-looking flags.

The whole thing might feel as distant to him as it does to me when I read a museum plaque explaining that, eight centuries ago, the Chola Dynasty, whose flag featured a leaping tiger on a saffron field, fought a series of bloody campaigns against the Srivijaya Empire, defenders of a royal Buddhist order. Their conflict, I'm told, was "over control of Indian Ocean trade routes." I accept that. I don't have much expertise to question the summary, and no emotional reason to try.

But I also know that if some future museum were to describe the Cold War of the 20th century as "a series of violent proxy wars over resource access in the post-colonial period, waged by the two largest remaining military powers after the world wars," I'd find myself wincing. Sure, that's not *wrong*. But it flattens everything. It leaves out the emotional texture, the moral fervor, the ideological conviction that millions lived and died for. It would feel foreign. Maybe even offensive.

Not that there's anything wrong with insulting people who are convinced they're too morally complex to be reduced to an overly simplistic and mistaken plaque. Living through a historical moment doesn't guarantee that you understand it any better than someone reading about it centuries later. If anything, your closeness might have warped your view. Future observers might see things more clearly than you ever could, especially when it comes to *moral judgment*.

And they *will* judge you, whether you like it or not. But they will be more like you than they realize. Their moral clarity about the 20th Century Wars will feel righteous and settled. But they'll be navigating the same internal battles, the same longing for moral integrity, the same improvisations toward moral belonging, and the same fragile hope that history might eventually explain it all.

In fact, the essence of our own moral struggles aren't any different from those of the righteous, fighting Chola adorned in golden chains, whom I casually shrugged at a few paragraphs ago. That recognition, that identical moral echo across time, is part of the case I'll be making in the chapters ahead.

But first, we need to stay with history a little longer because it's not just hard to hold, it's hard to trust.

Expertise and the Historian Imitation Game

The question of the "factual truth" of history is not one that I am going to take incredibly seriously in this book. You have likely gathered that I am not a historian. I'm a philosopher, a filmmaker, and a storyteller, interested in morality, existentialism, psychology, and the ways we make meaning. But I love history. You do too, I suspect. I love the strange characters, the broken monuments, the feeling that the world used to be different and somehow still is.

I probably get my history from the same places you do. Books, documentaries, museums, podcasts, conversations with older relatives, and increasingly, from clicking through links in Wikipedia rabbit holes or interrogating LLM chatbots (don't worry — I demand sources). This is how most of us absorb "history." And it's likely how most historians do it as well, though they are supposed to make a better effort than you or me to get down to "primary sources" to validate, defend, confirm, discover, or revise whatever historical narrative they are positing. I will leave that expertise up to them.

But I won't spare them from my moral analysis. There seem to be some fantastic historians, and some not-so-fantastic.

A fantastic historian, in my view, is not just someone who memorizes a mountain of dates and footnotes. It's someone who has learned how to be a historian. Because there's a difference. Learning about a set of events is not the same as learning how to live inside the limits of evidence, to acknowledge the gaps, the mediation, the moral weight behind what gets emphasized and what gets left out.

Let me show you what I mean.

An hour ago, I knew very little about Han Feizi, the 4th-century BCE Chinese philosopher whose Legalist ideas would help shape the Qin Dynasty's notoriously ruthless statecraft. I didn't know he had a rival, Li Si, another court advisor who would eventually convince the emperor to adopt strict Legalist reforms. I didn't know that after Han Feizi was accused of treason, likely with Li Si's encouragement, he was forced to commit suicide, probably by poison. Nor did I know that, just two decades later, those same reforms would culminate in the infamous campaigns to burn the books of scholars (213–211 BCE), after the campaign to burn the bodies of scholars (212–210 BCE).

But here I am now, casually laying all this out, simply because I looked it up. A BBC article from 2012, a journal of library history from the '70s, and a Britannica summary were enough to get me here. That's not nothing. But what I've just done is a performance, an imitation of authority using tools that are widely available. And it won't be the last time I do that.

This doesn't make me a historian. It just makes me an attentive reader with decent prose.

And I wonder, does that make you a little nervous? Do you worry that I might not be trustworthy enough to deliver "history" to you? If so, I get it. I share that nervousness. I'm trying to handle it responsibly and do good research. I'm leaning on the work of others who have supposedly earned more credibility than I have in these domains. If something I write turns out to be wrong, maybe we can both blame the historians I read. But that feeling, the sense that "history should be left to the experts," is worth pausing on. It speaks to the intuition that history is a powerful thing, a *dangerous* thing, maybe even a *sacred* thing.

In fact, access to historical knowledge has often been the exclusive domain of religious authorities. From Egyptian priests (c. 3000–1000 BCE) who curated dynastic records as part of divine order, to medieval Christian monks (6th–14th centuries) who preserved the past in Latin behind monastery walls, to Islamic scholars of the Golden Age (8th–13th centuries) who interpreted history through legal and moral frameworks, and to Jewish rabbis (3rd–6th centuries CE) who shaped communal memory through Talmudic law. All were deeply concerned with how the past could guide or control their moral and political present; and the irony, of course, is that I assembled all of that from research that took fifteen minutes.

The religious orders knew that history can *radicalize*. And that digesting historical knowledge can cause a collapse of meaning and a crisis of moral justification for any hierarchical structure which the top of said structure would rather keep intact.

Politically authoritarian regimes have always known this as well. They rewrite and hide history, or resurrect specific strands of it. Maybe that's why we give doctorates to historians. Maybe it's why we treat historical authority as something sacred, or maybe we should. But as I've noted, the informational cat is out of the bag.

We live in a strange moment, maybe a fleeting one, where access to historical knowledge is wide open, relatively unregulated, and weirdly intimate. We might be in a short-lived sweet spot. Some new form of censorship or intellectual lockdown may be coming. I fear that it likely is.

But I do know that, for now, my imitation of a historian is probably pretty good and yours would be too ... and so would your neighbors' ... and your friends' ... and your enemies'. And that fact is both exciting and terrifying. Because imitating a historian is one thing, but imitating a good moral philosopher is not something that I would recommend. There is no faking it when it comes to moral integrity. But that argument will wait for future chapters.

First, let's get back to a more existential layer of the question of trustworthy historical sources. If historical truth is always mediated, always layered, what does it mean to get as close as possible to the ground floor of truth? What is a "primary source" in the most personal, undeniable, and philosophical sense? What do we really undeniably *know*?

The Sensation Horizon

Right now, as I write these words, things are unfolding in the world.

I'm sitting in a beautiful research library in Madrid, Spain. There are names carved in gold above the marble frieze: R.JIM DERADA, FRAN SUAREZ, QUINTANA. I don't know who any of them are. Somewhere else, a president is on a secure line. A glacier is cracking. A microbe is drifting through the air. Fighters are filming TikToks from trench lines, and rebels are painting colors onto flags.

Me? I'm watching a woman in a purple sweater walk past my desk. Her shoes squeak. A man scratches his ear. She returns a moment later, but I don't see her, I just hear the steps. I imagine it's her. Do I *know* she is there?

All truth is mediated and filtered, even the woman in purple's steps. The steps are no longer sensations in the present. They are memories, composed mostly of visual and auditory impressions, and already they are slipping into the territory of symbol and reconstruction.

Memories can be faulty. Wait, was it a sweater or a button-down blouse? And what happened during the time she was out of my view? I don't *know*. I could ask the librarian. Maybe she remembers. Maybe she could check the computer log. Is that "true"? Sure, true *enough* for me. And honestly, not much moral weight hangs on that particular chain of evidence.

But the same questions become much more serious when I try to understand something beyond my immediate experience. For example, what's happening right now in negotiations between Russia and Ukraine over the Donbas region? I could read several news outlets. I could couple that with some history books about the region. But I know, without cynicism, just with realism, that every layer of that information is soaked in mediation, memory, bias, framing, politics, and contradiction. And yet, I feel compelled to accept some level of "truth" about it. Because what's the alternative? Not knowing anything at all?

This is where I admit I'm being a little "philosopherish." Forgive me. I'm being a stickler for, maybe too much, the raw nature of truth. But it's important that I am, at least for a moment. I'm not arguing that all truth is inaccessible or unknowable. I'm not interested in the kind of floating relativism that denies all meaning of truth. I'm just trying to draw our attention to the fact that, when it comes to something as powerful as history, we would be wise to remember the layers.

There really is such a thing as a sensation horizon, a boundary beyond which all information becomes mediated. Within that horizon, there is only your own immediate and subjective experience, in real time. Philosophers of mind have a word for this undeniably subjective consciousness stuff. The world is qualia. And a full debate and consideration of the philosophical soundness of the idea belongs in other books. But I wanted to put my "philosopher" cards on the table and announce that we should recognize that the moment something moves beyond the sensation horizon, into memory, description, recording, or secondhand report, it gains a layer. That layer can take many forms. Photographs, eyewitness accounts, scientific data, journalistic reporting. But each one introduces a question of trust. By the time a piece of "news," let alone "history," hits us, it is cloaked in many layers.

And so I've taken this short existential detour to get us back to the questions of those whose job it is to narrate the world to us, the journalists, the historians, and the philosophers. These are the interpreters of the waves which are made up ultimately of the raw sensations of others. And while we may not be able to live without them, we should ask what tools they're using, what stories they're telling, and what truths they may be smoothing over in the process.

Chapter 2

Fact Wranglers, Theory Stitchers, and Rug Pullers

The Dance of Moral Distortion Between Journalists, Historians, and Philosophers

Smuggling Morality Through Neutrality

There's a familiar line that "journalists write the first draft of history." It's clever but misleading. The real distinction between journalism and history is philosophical, not chronological.

In a perfectly ordered world, journalists would tell us *what* happened. Historians try to tell us *why* it did. And moral philosophers? We don't just ask *what* happened or *why*, it's our job to ask what *ought to* have happened. That's a far more explosive job, but it's one we're all wrestling with. So we may as well get better at it.

Now, in our very messy world, journalists often sneak into the historian's closet, wrap themselves in narrative, and sell it as neutral reporting. And everyone carries a moral philosophy with them whether they are aware of it or not. The word choice, the framing, the passive constructions, the convenient omissions, none of it is morally innocent. And if you're not watching closely, they'll instruct you on how you should morally slot certain events while pretending they're just telling you what happened.

But even if a journalist somehow manages to report a fact morally neutrally, our brains won't leave it there. We can't help ourselves. We slot. We interpret. Immediately. Automatically. We humans are habitual narrative detectives.

In my work as a documentary editor and filmmaker, I have become tremendously familiar with the trick. Documentary is a strange art form. It's suspended somewhere between journalism and narrative storytelling. My artistic raw materials, in neutral terms, are sequential frames of light and sound captured in unscripted moments.

Let's say I have four shots to work with: a woman sleeping alone in a messy queen-sized bed at noon with the window open on a snowy day, a dog leash being dropped by a muddy welcome mat, a close-up of a subway car door opening, and a wedding ring being placed in a pawn shop display case. Depending on how I sequence those four images, how long I let each linger, what kind of music I layer underneath, your brain will begin stitching a particular story. It won't be optional. You'll build a moral narrative theory. Or more likely, several theories, in real time.

And the "fun" of watching is seeing which theories rise or fall in probability as I offer more evidence. Maybe the next shot is a man walking a dog along the train tracks with a brand-new leash. Suddenly you're wondering: What happened in that subway car? Whose wedding ring was it? Are they coming back? Who are the good guys and bad guys? If I conduct a test screening and catch a focus group thinking about the subway car *too much* in a way that is distracting, maybe I omit that shot on a reedit, or perhaps I *wanted* it to be a mental lure as a kind of emotional red herring.

Heck, even I want to know what happened to that lady, and I was the one who literally just made those images up. We can't help it. This is what humans do. And it's no different when the unslotted material is called "the news."

Let me show you.

Palestinian children are being incinerated by Israeli bombs.

Stop. Read it again and watch your brain for ten seconds.

If you have even a half-formed moral opinion on the Israel-Palestine conflict, that sentence won't stay as a neutral fact. It triggers a morally laden explanatory theory.

Maybe your mind jumped to "unfortunate collateral damage." Maybe to "ethnic cleansing." Maybe to "genocide." Maybe to "human shields." Either way, your "why" came pre-loaded, and it wasn't morally neutral nor could it have been absent of historical framings.

Let's slow that down for a bit. That one sentence — *Children are being incinerated by Israeli bombs* — sets off a mental chain reaction.

First, the journalist in your mind logs it. *What* happened. A snapshot is taken. As gruesome as the image is, it's fairly plain.

Then the journalist passes that snapshot to the historian. The historian doesn't change the picture, but starts building the frame. Maybe they write something on it. A date. A name. A string of causes. If you know any background, your mind might already be engraving things in the frame: "this was retaliation," or "a continuation of a larger land grab campaign," or "rooted in decades of displacement and failed diplomacy." Maybe you reach for "1917," or "1948," or "1967," or "Oslo," or "October 7th," or "the collapse of a recent ceasefire negotiation." The historian gives the event a before and after. The frame starts to take shape. It has logic and rationale, even if it's messy and contested. Then the framed image is handed off again. This time to the moral philosopher in your mind.

The philosopher looks at it, considers the angle, and decides where to shelve it. Where to display it in the moral museum in your mind. Which moral theory does it belong to? What category does it fall under? Is it justice, injustice, necessity, atrocity? The philosopher is doing the final sorting.

The philosopher reads the frame and the historian's handiwork. Then he turns to the shelves he's built over time, each one categorized to a different moral framework. Utilitarianism. Consequentialism. Deontology. Virtue ethics. Divine command. (We'll explore these more closely in the next chapter.) The philosopher places it on the shelf. That's the final sorting. And although we're breaking it down slowly here, in reality the entire process happens in a blink.

Is it possible for a historical narrative to not strongly suggest what moral framework you should, or most reasonably should, slot the event into? I'm not sure. But I'm also not too concerned with whether it can be fully neutral or morally ambivalent. We all really are moral philosophers at every step.

But even if you don't know any relevant history about the particular sentence I offered, if the same sentence had referenced very real violence in the jungles of the Central African Republic, for instance, your mind would still try to morally shelve it. *Children are being hacked to death by militia fighters in the Central African Republic.* Your historian who knows very little about the relevant pasts of that issue might shrug and simply hand the snapshot straight to the philosopher. The context would be thinner, the slotting more uncertain. It might feel like a blur, even if the moral weight is just as heavy.

This is the triangle: journalist, historian, philosopher, and it lives inside every one of us. We take in the fact, we search for the reason, and we try to decide if we're okay with it. We do it instinctively and constantly. The trouble is, we rarely do it carefully or without a dreadful tangle of psychological self-preservation, fear, and bias.

And recently, the sequence isn't just getting messy. It is being hijacked. What should be a careful mental handoff from journalist to historian to philosopher has become a scrambled assembly line.

Journalists, the ones who are supposed to capture and present the raw image, now blur the lens and deliver theory disguised as fact. Headlines are crafted to smuggle moral cues straight into your interpretation. Historians are either sidelined or dragged directly into live political battles, made to frame events before they've even cooled. And moral philosophers are ignored or shouted down for asking the questions that make the whole machine stall.

The tension that once held this mental triangle together has snapped. And nowhere is that more obvious than in the modern spectacle of breaking news.

Breaking Us

It was late in the evening in 1991. I was eight years old, playing Zelda II on our new Super Nintendo. I was slain again on my quest to save the princess, and it was nearing my bedtime anyway. I pressed the power button and the game blipped off, giving way to the live television. I was about to turn that off as well, but then I saw it. That bold graphic, big block letters spinning dramatically into place as alarm bell music orchestra hits leapt from the speaker like syncopated trumpets, BREAKING NEWS.

Before the graphic even finished a partial rotation I was already calling out to the entire house. "Mom! Dad! Something's happening!" I was a very astute eight-year-old. I had probably only seen this graphic once or twice in my life. Maybe the Exxon Valdez Oil Spill? Maybe the fall of the Berlin Wall? *Something* definitely was happening, and these journalists were about to tell me.

My dad rushed over. We both stared at the screen. The anchor shuffled papers. Everyone looked serious. His tone was as heavy as his script, "Good evening. We have some major breaking news at this hour from the Middle East..." Then came the blurry green night-vision footage of glowing missiles streaking upward into the night. January 16th, 1991. The Persian Gulf War had begun.

It was a *real* moment. It felt like "history."

Now fast-forward two decades through the explosion of cable and Internet newsfeeds, to just a few years ago. I checked CNN's website and saw that the big bold red *Breaking News* banner was stamped across the entire thing. This must be huge news akin to something like a war starting, right? No, it was a story announcing the death of Norm Macdonald.

And listen, I think Norm Macdonald was a brilliant comedian and I hope future readers, who very likely won't find his name in a history book, go ahead and dig into the video archives and binge on his genius comedy. But it's not exactly the fall of the Berlin Wall.

Imagine if I had yelled for my parents with the same urgency? Only to deliver that update? I'm sure there aren't any eight-year-olds today who are shaken into hysterics by the suggestion that there is a "Breaking News" graphic leading into a report.

I've tried to find data on just how much more frequently the phrase *"Breaking News"* appears on screens compared to when I was a kid, but there doesn't seem to be a comprehensive study, at least not yet. Still, anecdotally, it feels like the frequency has increased by something like a million percent (roughly). When I was eight, you might see that graphic once a year. Now, if you go twenty-four hours without it flashing across your screen, it feels like something's wrong with the world, or the algorithm.

This is the natural logic of competition in the attention economy, amplified by the design of social media and 24/7 content pipelines. News outlets aren't simply reporting, they're competing. Every headline is tuned to trip the wire of urgency. Every image, every word, is trying to grab you by the collar and insist, *this matters more than everything else.* But the result is that something important has eroded. The journalist, historian, philosopher triangle was always fragile. But now it's fraying under the weight of financial incentives, engagement metrics, and moral overload. And I think that's a problem for all of us.

I'll have more to say about the attention economy and its role in enforcing and supporting a neoliberal utilitarian moral framework in later chapters. But it deserved a brief nod here, if only to acknowledge how hard it has become to distinguish between *what happened* and *why it happened* and what *ought to have*.

A Quick Aside on the Elephant in the Book

You've probably noticed by now that I've referred — more than once — to one of the most morally radioactive, politically polarizing, and historically overworked topics in modern memory: Israel and Palestine. I want to address that directly before you turn the page. There are a few reasons.

First, I have some personal experience with this issue that has shaped the way I think about history, identity, and justice. Second, I don't believe the intense focus on this conflict is accidental, or the result of some supernatural force like global antisemitism. I think it's a by-product of something very real. This conflict sits at a uniquely overloaded intersection of religion, empire, memory, security, resistance, and global narrative control. It's the place where so many unresolved tensions in the world, colonial guilt, theological arrogance, nationalist trauma, identity politics, even a racial dominance dynamic, get poured, often unconsciously, into a single, burning vessel.

For many, it becomes an avatar for *everything* that feels off or upside down in the modern world. And because it's such a messy convergence of traumas and imperatives, it's also a perfect pressure-test for the themes of this book.

So yes, I *will* reference it again. Not because I want to be provocative or try to solve it, but because it shows us what happens when moral frameworks collide with living history. I hope, wherever you stand (or don't) on this issue, you'll understand why I think it matters.

And on that note, to explain how historical facts often cannot litigate moral positions on their own:

The Rothschild Riddle

History cannot tell us what *ought* to have happened. It can only show us what *did*. And from there, we're left with a puzzle: how do we assign moral meaning to events which seem to fold back upon themselves in a kind of causality loop? For this, the story of the Rothschild family in the late 19th and early 20th century is a perfect case study.

As antisemitism flared across Europe and nationalist movements gained steam, Jews, along with many other ethnic and religious minorities, faced both a moral and strategic question. How to survive, and what kind of world was worth pursuing. Among the Jewish elite, no family had more options, or more influence, than the Rothschilds. Ironically, their wealth itself was a historical by-product of exclusion and discrimination. For centuries, restrictive laws in Europe barred Jews from owning land or entering many professions, inadvertently funneling many of them into finance, trade, and banking roles. The Rothschilds became trusted with wealth partly because, as second-tier citizens, even tremendously wealthy ones, they were seen as less able to cheat those in power. By the turn of the 20th century, they had vast resources, global reach, and diverging theories on what Jewish survival ought to look like.

The first theory would be represented by Nathan Rothschild in London. He believed that the safest path forward for Jews was assimilation. He saw Jewish integration into European society through loyalty, cultural alignment, and economic success as the best defense against antisemitism. He deeply feared that overt political Zionism would provoke even more hatred and suspicion. To Nathan, calls for a Jewish homeland risked reinforcing the accusation of dual loyalty. He famously wrote, "We are Englishmen. Let us stay Englishmen." For him, safety meant thriving in the nations where Jews already lived, not declaring their separateness.

The second theory could be represented by Edmund de Rothschild in Paris. While he did not support the overt declarations of political Zionism, he quietly funded Jewish agricultural settlements in Palestine. His goal was refuge, not statehood. He purchased land north of Jerusalem from absentee Christian landlords like the Sursock family, hoping to create safe havens for Jews facing persecution in Eastern Europe and Russia. However, most of these land transfers displaced

Palestinian Arabs who had farmed the land for generations. Legal disputes followed but the soon-to-be-defunct Ottoman Empire upheld the purchases. Edmund, at least nominally, encouraged the settlers he supported to hire and coexist peacefully with the native population. We can speculate that these modest suggestions were a mixture of ensuring a safe environment and some moral consideration to the displaced locals. He seemed to believe that Jewish survival might require physical relocation from Europe, but not domination, not nationalism, and certainly not statehood.

The third theory was aggressive and overt political Zionism as represented by figures like Theodor Herzl, and more strongly his successors in Chaim Weizmann. They rejected both assimilation and passive relocation. They argued that Jews would never be safe until they had sovereignty and a state of their own. To them, antisemitism was not a fringe phenomenon, but a recurring feature of European life. They believed that the world's refusal to accept Jews as full citizens made assimilation a dangerous fantasy. They set their sights on Palestine (after being encouraged by the British to take a serious look at the Uganda/Kenya border which seemed less inhabited and politically fraught).

By 1917, their position had gained major traction. That year, Nathan's son, Walter Rothschild, who had adopted the theory of the aggressive Zionism of Herzl and Weizmann, became the recipient of the Balfour Declaration, a letter from the British government publicly endorsing the establishment of a Jewish homeland in Palestine. The dream of a sovereign Jewish state was beginning to materialize; the native population was merely an obstacle which would need to be taken care of in whatever way possible as a form of collateral damage. The theory presented little moral choice in the matter.

And the tragic irony is that looking back, all three positions, European assimilation, coexistent refuge-building, and exclusionary aggressive Jewish-nationalism and statehood pursuit (Zionism), can use "history" to claim some measure of vindication. The rise of Nazism and the targeting of Jews and many other ethno-religious groups in Europe gave the Zionists *their* terrible support, "assimilation was always a false dream and they had 'no choice' but to be violent Jewish-nationalists and supremacists." But for assimilationists, the very ascendance of antisemitic Nazism was the "backlash" to Zionism they had warned about decades earlier and the violence and charges of "dual loyalty" that followed confirmed *their* deepest fears. Meanwhile, the aggressively anti-Arab settler-colonial Zionist patterns that emerged in Palestine provided argumentative ammunition for the initial fears of Edmund and *his* emphasis on peaceful integration and shared nationhood with the native Palestinian population rather than political domination.

Each accusatory camp gets to look at the mess today and the ugly sentence about Israeli bombs and Palestinian children and proclaim, "I told you so!" And the morally defensive camp who seems to be closest aligned with the status quo (Zionism) also gets to say, "This isn't what we meant!"

That's the problem with litigating morality through history. We only have the path that *did* happen. And no matter how it unfolded, someone will always argue that another path would have been better or worse. We lean on history to prove our point, but we do it by imagining counterfactual worlds: *If only they had listened to Herzl sooner ... If only they hadn't provoked the antisemites ... If only they'd stayed quiet, or left earlier, or stayed behind ... If only they hadn't oppressed the Palestinians.*

You can play this game with *any* moment in history. You can rerun the tape in your mind, tweak a few decisions, and invent a cleaner moral ending. And *everyone else can too.*

The facts of history are real, and they matter. But they are not as helpful as we want them to be in settling moral debates.

Because the moment you use a historical outcome to justify a moral stance, someone else will build a different counterfactual to justify the opposite.

What this shows us is that ***moral philosophy must come first***. History can illustrate. It can warn. It can inspire. But it cannot tell us what was right on its own. It cannot answer for us what *ought* to have happened. Only we can do that. If we don't start with philosophy, we'll just keep scavenging through history for the stories that protect our anxious psyches.

Morality as a Form of Interpreting Truth

Before we end our initial contemplation on history and move into Chapter 3 where you will meet the villain who's already been whispering in your mind, I want to linger on one final moment, a small but revealing public exchange that, in its awkward phrasing and backlash, accidentally sums up the entire tension we've been circling.

Alexandria Ocasio-Cortez made an ear-catching comment during a 2019 interview on *60 Minutes*. When challenged about the accuracy of one of her statements regarding what she contended was mismanaged and immoral government spending, she said, "I think there's a lot of people more concerned about being precisely, factually, and semantically correct than about being morally right."

Critics like Ben Shapiro (no relation, by the way) seized on this, arguing that moral arguments require factual accuracy to hold weight. He quipped, "You can't be morally correct if you're factually wrong." This critique resonated with the Internet, as a lot of egoistic drama does.

But I think AOC inadvertently opened an important question. What is the relationship between "truth" and moral frameworks? Facts alone do not dictate morality. They require moral interpretation to gain meaning. That requires a framework to contextualize it, to weigh its significance against our values and principles. In this way, every fact is morally interpreted, even when we don't consciously realize it.

I know I am likely giving both Ocasio-Cortez and Shapiro far too much credit here. Neither seemed to fully articulate this, and they were certainly not trying to engage in a philosophical debate. But the tension between AOC's "morally right" and Shapiro's "factually correct" highlights how facts, on their own, are never enough; they must be stitched into narratives and filtered through values to become morally significant.

By combining their two stakes in this little spat, AOC's push for moral urgency and Shapiro's demand for factual precision, we land on a far more interesting question. Is there any such thing as a *moral fact* at all? That's not something we can answer quickly. It deserves a chapter of its own, and it will get one. But for now, let's let their tension settle into the soil. It fertilizes the friction between "truth," "story," and "judgment" which is the darkness from which, in the next chapter, our villain finally steps into the light.

What Historical Fiction and This Symbol ~~~ Are Doing in This Book

To take a coherent and comprehensive view of the relationship between morality and history, we have to populate it with sensations. We must imagine ourselves into the lives of past others, not just their actions, but their thoughts, their fears, and the stories they told themselves. This (~~~) is my attempt to be fair to the people of the past.

One day, we'll be the ones on trial. Some future moral thinker will likely look back at the grand narratives of our time: the climate crisis, global inequality, technological upheaval, economically incentivized genocides, massively destructive "dumb" bombs, and massively misused "smart" bombs, pandemic policies. They will pity, scold, or applaud us due to future political factors beyond our control.

But when they look at us as individuals, will they see our sensations? Will they understand the tension of our lives, the love we felt, the compromises we made, the contradictions we inherited, the things we dreamt about in the quiet moments? I hope they'll try.

That's what I want for the people of the past too. So, when you see this symbol ~~~, you'll know you're about to step into a moment imagined from that imperfect wave of history. Consider it an engraved invitation to a very cool moral time machine that I've built for you.

I've researched these scenes carefully and pieced them together from the best evidence I could find. They're filtered through the historians at my fingertips and they remain interpretations. I hope they make you feel something. I hope they make you think of your own life. I hope they make you consider the question, what would someone in the future need to know about you to judge you fairly? What would you want them to understand?

And remember, your *former self* is a person just like those past others. You can freeze your past decisions and situations and build them into dioramas in a mental museum. You can gaze through the glass down at them and pity, scold, or applaud just as easily.

I hope the following chapters will help us all do that with more honesty, kindness, fairness, and most of all, moral courage.

Chapter 3

The Moral Stalemate

Why moral philosophy is stuck in a rut and how to break free of the tug-of-war of politics

In Case of Moral Emergency, Break Glass

You'd think we'd have better tools by now.

Millennia of moral philosophers, centuries of revolutions, decades of self-help books, and still, most of us are trying to make ethical decisions with something like a broken compass, a foggy windshield, or the wrong map altogether.

I'm not here to give you perfect topography or an unerring GPS. Instead, I'm going to hand you two instruments, imperfect, slightly suspect tools for navigating the moral wilderness. One comes from the world of psychology and is something like a flashlight, something that helps you notice and detect subtle shifts in how your beliefs adapt to pressure. The other comes from the world of moral philosophy and is more like a wobbly scale, trying to weigh out principles versus consequences.

I could just explain these tools to you, of course. I could write it all down in clean textbook terms and march you through the diagrams like a college seminar. But I think it would be much more fun, and far more honest to the spirit of this book, which insists that the root of moral life begins in sensation, not abstraction, if I tried to get you to *feel* these tools first. Not in theory. In action. And besides, I went to great lengths to build this moral time machine. So, we may as well put it to good use.

Don't worry too much about the design; think of your favorite sci-fi movie and reduce the budget to pen and ink and daydreams. It can whisk us to any time. The machine has some limitations, of course. I bought it from a disgruntled philosopher who couldn't guarantee that it wasn't really just a simulation machine which was generating worlds based on the faulty memories of filtered and biased historians and journalists. There really is no way to tell if what you experience while inside the machine is just springing from the imagination of a well-read, movie loving, modestly talented writer in the early 21st century working on a book about moral philosophy, or if it is actually bringing you to historical slices of the universe. We're just going to have to trust the exercise together. Besides, it's a free ride.

So, go ahead. Step in and get comfortable. I have two exciting destinations dialed in for you. I'll close the door and pull the lever to send you off to the first one. Enjoy.

Stop One: Clockwise to Nowhere

~~~

Before you is a simple square-shaped board resting on a table. There are rectangular wooden pegs affixed to the thing pointing up at you, all standing in neat little rows on a grid. It looks like something cobbled together by a sophomoric shop class flunky who was practicing measurements. You inspect the thing to see if there is more to it, anything that might hint at some kind of excitement. Perhaps it's a kind of chess type game with hidden strategies? Nope. It's just a pegboard. Well, that's what you get for blindly signing up for a psychology experiment.

Welcome to Leon Festinger's blandly painted psychology department on the Stanford University campus in the year 1959. (I promise you that our time machine has much more compelling destinations in store for us. But this one is important. Trust me.)

After a few moments, graduate student James Carlsmith enters the room holding a clipboard. He looks precisely like you'd expect a graduate student named James Carlsmith holding a clipboard in 1959 to look. He sets a timer down on the table as he takes a seat across from you. This isn't getting any better.

"Thank you for agreeing to participate in the study today. Let me explain the task you'll be partaking in. Do you see how the pegs affixed to the board in front of you can be rotated on their axis?"

You nod.
~~~

"Okay, great. So, I want you to start at the top left; turn that peg counterclockwise, a quarter turn. And then proceed to the next peg below that one and do the same. And the next, and so on. Once you have turned all the pegs on the board, I'd like you to reverse the process and turn each of them clockwise back to their original position, one by one. Once they are back in that position, you will repeat the process. I'd like you to do this for an hour."

He starts a timer and watches. Get turning, buddy.

After you consider pulling the fire alarm and running away, you begrudgingly begin turning the pegs. After an hour of dragging your hands and numbed mind through this monotonous "game" while James simply watches, the merciful chime of the timer finally releases you from your boredom. Now James has just a few questions for you.

He asks you how enjoyable you found the task, if you found it interesting or boring, and if you'd be willing to participate in similar studies.

Is he kidding? If you could give *negative* stars in the rating, you would. This whole thing was a complete waste of an hour in your view. Perhaps you had a few moments where you tried to convince yourself that this was a kind of rosary beads or Zen rock garden meditation practice. But you could have done that on your *own* time back at the dorm room. You didn't need James and his seemingly unnecessary stale white lab coat to be involved.

You offer your overwhelming negative reviews to James as he records your answers and thanks you for being a part of this groundbreaking study. Confused, and slightly annoyed, you exit the lab.

Okay, before you demand the time machine whisk you to somewhere more exciting, let's go back in and watch the two important variations of the experiment. I had placed you, perhaps more mercifully than you now realize, as a part of the "control group" of the study. You did great, by the way.

Another student who is unknowingly in "Experimental Group 1" takes a seat across from James. The whole thing starts with the same sequence of events. The student is asked to "play" the pegboard game for a dreadfully boring hour. James simply watches, just as he did for you. But after the hour concludes we see the wrinkle. There are no survey questions about the enjoyment of the activity, quite yet.

James tells the student that he has a request. He says that there is another student in the waiting room who is also about to participate in the study. That student will soon be doing precisely the same peg exercise. Normally, the lab has an assistant out there in the waiting room who prepares the student for the activity by telling them how *interesting*, *exciting*, and *fun* the exercise is. But the assistant is running late today. James asks if the participant wouldn't mind filling in and preparing the next student by telling them that stuff about how fun it is going to be. Oh, and the lab will offer $20 for the trouble. How about it?

The student's eyes perk up. (Keep in mind that adjusted for inflation that $20 would be about $220 today. And we are talking about college students here. $220 still buys a lot of ramen noodles. In terms of purchasing power, $20 dollars in 1959 was close to the average of a month of rent in a shared room for a college student.) The student shrugs, takes the cash, and replies that he'd be happy to help out.

He then goes out to the waiting room where a lonely student awaits by an empty chair. Our now moderately richer student sits next to him and proceeds to gush about the rather "interesting" and "exciting" task that the lucky newcomer is about to enjoy. He does this for a few more students over the course of an hour, each time explaining how fun the thing is going to be. Eventually, James comes out to inform him that the lab assistant has finally arrived. He is relieved of his prepping job.

But before he goes, he has to answer some simple questions. He is given the same three questions as you got about enjoyment, recommendation, and boringness levels of the peg-turning task. And his answers are generally in line with yours, only slightly inflated. But he reports that he *really* found the task pretty boring. He's not so keen on doing anything like it again. And he didn't enjoy it too much. All of this runs counter to the glowing review he was just giving to the waiting students.

I trust that this behavior is not much of a mystery to you. Twenty bucks *is* twenty bucks. But the real discovery happens with "Experimental Group 2." Let's watch as a participating student unknowingly in that group enters the lab.

We see the same initial procedure. The student goes through the same boring peg turning for an hour and is presented with the same request to fill in for a tardy lab assistant to prepare the next students with a positive pep talk. The only difference here is that the student is offered much less money for the job. They are offered only $1 (that dollar could swing for a movie ticket in 1959 or a burger and fries or a few gallons of gas). It's not *nothing*, but it's not going to change anyone's life.

This student thinks about the $1 offer for a bit, a small twist of the lower lip, and a squint, and then agrees.

The student is handed the crisp dollar bill and then heads off to the waiting room and proceeds with the preparatory adoration to a waiting student. After a few more of these talks with incoming students, James comes out to release him but first, again, he asks this student to answer the same three questions about the enjoyment of pegboard turning. And this is where things get *really* interesting.

This student answers that they *genuinely enjoyed* the pegboard task. They really found a lot of scientific value in the experiment, and they'd happily participate in something like it again. The answers are serious and well thought out. The student really discovered a lot of value and *fun* in all that turning. The pegboard game was suddenly getting smashing reviews from students in the $1 dollar group.

Could it be that the students who were put into that group just all randomly have wildly mild motor skill task fetishes? What the heck is going on here?

Cognitive Dissonance: Cheap Lies and Expensive Truths

Cognitive dissonance is one of the most resurgent terms in online discourse in recent years. It's slung around on social media platforms as an intellectual-sounding arrow aiming to vanquish an online agitator. It's almost always misunderstood by the archers themselves.

Cognitive dissonance is a feeling, a bad one, an itchy one, an uncomfortable one. Cognitive dissonance feels like an unpleasant mental tension or unease that happens when we hold conflicting beliefs, values, or attitudes. It's a persistent, nagging discomfort in our minds, pushing us to resolve the inconsistency by changing our thoughts or behaviors to relieve the internal conflict. This "mental friction" is what Festinger surmised must be producing so many wooden peg turning fans in Experimental Group 2.

Nearly all of us have a very important belief in our minds that contends that "I am a good person." Think of this as a gear that turns in lock step with other gears. The "I'm a good person" gear is central and large. If that gear jams, the whole elaborate machinery breaks in a rather catastrophic way. Most of us also have another belief-gear that reads, "Lying is bad." (Note here that I am being careful to choose the word "bad" here, rather than "wrong.")

Let's zoom into the mind of our friend who has accepted the $1 as he sits down to gush about the exciting wooden pegs. In his mind, the "Lying is bad" gear is starting to turn; and in turn the gear next to it which says "good people don't do bad things" gets moving. But that gear is interlocked to the very important central "I'm a good person" belief-gear. This "good people don't do bad things" gear is jamming it up, grinding it, resisting the flow. That hurts. And *that* is cognitive dissonance.

Festinger then takes the next logical step by asserting that this situation is unbearable. It's a printer jam of the highest degree. And something must be fixed to get the machine moving again. Your mind makes an urgent phone call.

The Repairman Cometh

Remember the villain I warned you about in the introduction? Well, here he comes.

Toolbox in hand, wearing a wrinkled polo, he enters with soft footsteps. He's here to save the day, or at least to make the discomfort stop.

He opens up his kit, stuffed not with wrenches or screwdrivers but with memos, rationalizations, motivational posters, public relations drafts, a half-written op-ed, some tweets, a few dusty Supreme Court dissents, and a sticky note that says, "just pivot." This man is prepared.

Let's first send our Repair guy over to the $20 dollar group, because you could argue that this same gear jam might have occurred there. And it definitely did, though the Repairman was barely needed. It was all obvious, and sounded like this, "Well, yeah, this love fest for the pegboard that you are telling the student is basically a lie, and lying is bad, sure. But twenty bucks is twenty bucks! Are you kidding me? It's not *that* bad. And everyone does this kind of thing for money anyway. Chill. I mean, you can even donate a buck or two to charity. You're awesome." That's pretty much all that was needed to get things moving again. It was nearly automatic. The Repairman didn't even break a sweat. The reward, it appears, was sufficient to provide the *rationalization* for a moral infraction.

But over here in the $1 dollar mind, the deliberation over the jam is a bit more difficult. A good person *might* lie for $20 bucks, but just for $1? That doesn't really stick, and that repair job falls apart pretty quickly.

The Repairman might offer some other ideas like downplaying how big of an infraction this lie is, "I mean, come on, it's just some random student. What's the harm?" Or maybe they could try to resolve the jam with some fear tactic like, "You know, that James guy looked *pretty* dangerous actually. What if, and hear me out, you were just *afraid* of what he might do to you if you refused his offer? You were just really acting out of self-preservation which makes it totally morally permissible to lie!"

That repair job probably barely gets off the ground, especially because we're talking about the very non-dangerous James "pocket protector" Carlsmith.

So, after some moments of crisis and fear that the gears might all burst from their bolts, the Repairman comes up with a great idea. "I've got it! You see that gear right there that says, 'You are lying'? What if we just start turning that the other direction! You actually *loved* that peg game! Remember how cool it was to try to align them so precisely? It was kind of dull at first, sure, but you really grew to like it after a few minutes. You're all good here! You weren't *even* lying at all! You were telling these waiting students the truth! You are still a good person! Hurray!" And with that, the system is saved and the gears churn away smoothly. The Repairman pats himself on the back. Genius.

And that is the "Theory of Cognitive Dissonance."

This is what Festinger conjured up to explain the enjoyment survey results of Experimental Group 2. He called the specific phenomenon the *insufficient reward* and, as the title of my book suggests, I find it to be pretty darn important and hugely explanatory when applied to sociological and political trends.

We should be careful with the word "rationalize" as well. Because the important piece to take away from the insufficient reward discovery is that the people in this group do not consider their love of the pegboard to *be* a rationalization. They purport to believe that they enjoyed the peg turning when asked by the researcher. And who is to say that they are lying to themselves? The erased line between a genuinely held belief and a rationalization is the real discovery by Festinger. The "insufficient reward" group *really believes* they like turning pegs.

The $20 group is the one making a "rationalization" for the "immoral" behavior of lying in the study, and apparently, they are *aware* of that to some degree given their survey results. But the "insufficient reward" group? They *aren't* rationalizing, they are simply *believing*.

The takeaway is this, the most effective brainwasher of the mind is the mind's own desire to be moral, and sadly, the price tag on brainwashing is lower than most of us think. In fact, as the experiment demonstrates, the lower the price the more powerful the brainwashing actually is. Of course, if it goes *too* low, the student simply turns down the offer. There is a kind of range of "low, but not too low" insufficient rewards that has an awful gravitational attraction in capitalist logic that we will contend with in future chapters.

Now you have the first of two promised moral field instruments in hand, the psychological moral flashlight. This should help you detect the presence of the Repairman tinkering with the gears. It lets you notice when your thoughts are being adjusted in real time, under the surface, without your consultation. And now it's time to get you that second instrument from moral philosophy.

Back in the time machine.

The next stop isn't a lab. And while you may not have loved the pegboard, you might soon find yourself nostalgic for its boringness. The lever has been pulled.

Caught Between Right and Right

~~~

The smudged glass still visible between the heavy vinyl tarp curtains which once served as your crinkly shower curtain is hopelessly splattered with dust and caked mud, much more on the outside than the plane you can wipe clean from here. Not that you'd risk that kind of motion even if you had a cloth. You've been trying to remain quiet for months and display as few signs of life to the increasingly dangerous streets. Simply opening a window could invite deadly attention. But the red dust is too much. You need the view to the alleyway to be available, even if there is nothing to prepare. So, you take the chance, dampen a cloth, and unlatch the window pane and reach.

As you wipe, you hear the soft sounds of whispers hitching gentle rides on the hot air. You remember the vent installed in the false closet of what used to be your cousin's room, before he fled to the countryside like most of your other friends months ago. The architecture of the house made for a minor air stream which now carries voices, muffled prayers in the language of Arabic or Cham. You aren't sure. You don't speak either. For a moment though, serenity wins. The warmth and whispers are both okay as you scan the street.

You are in Phnom Penh, Cambodia. The year is 1976. And the sun is setting.

The normally active street is quiet, except for a brave street vendor still hoping to sell some used flatware from a rickety cart. He is of no concern, nor are the three yellow and brown puppies who play tug of war with a mess of fishing nets by the fluttering rubbish pile. You remember when their mother was pregnant with the litter. You used to leave a water dish by the door. The jumpy black birds still perch on phone wires above the street like they used to, and for a few seconds the soft melody of the
~~~

evening *maghrib* seems to punctuate their prancing claws like tap dancers or a nervous high wire act. You're confident that the prayers are only loud enough for you to hear, but still you think that you might want to go remind the family of Cham Muslims you've been secretly sheltering to keep it down, just in case.

You finish wiping the window and clasp it shut. And just like that, there's a glint of black metal rifles turning the corner. You swallow hard. The puppies scamper away without their toy. Where *did* their mother end up anyway?

The Khmer Rouge have been sweeping these areas for weeks now and have issued warnings about the harboring of enemies of the regime. They've made public edicts declaring the Cham Muslim population to be illegal, forcing them to eat pork, and abandon their cultural habits of dress, or even speak the Cham language. It goes without saying that harboring them secretly would result in immediate execution if you were lucky, brutal torture before the execution if you weren't. You do know some people who have successfully hidden and transported people, but, of course, it *is* a big risk. You also know some people who simply turned over the "enemies" and were spared, or even given rewards for their honesty, compliance, and aid to the regime. You *knew* all of this when you agreed to hide your neighbors, of course, but now the moment is arriving.

The kitchen suddenly feels much hotter. The humidity is settling on you like a second skin. Or maybe that is just your sweat. You know you must calm yourself if you have any chance of pulling this off. And so, you try to slow your breathing, even as you watch the always surprisingly young soldiers knock on the doors of abandoned houses across the way.

You carry yourself to the next room and swiftly to the closet where the family prays. When you open the door, no words need to be said. The father, whose name you have intentionally not learned precisely for fear of the coming moral decision, ceases his holy mumbling. He sees your sweat. He knows. His wife clutches the young boy closely as the three of them huddle in what may be precious time. The man nods as you both share a portion of deep gratitude for whatever may have happened and whatever will happen next, something you yourself are unsure of. You gently close the closet door.

Back in the kitchen, and now drying an already dry soup bowl, you wait for the knock. The soldiers' boots grind into gravel outside, each step scraping against your nerves. Everything far away is amplified and distorted. You can almost hear their static-crackle cigarette pulls as clearly as the clanking of their holsters. All you can do is steady your breath, one heartbeat at a time, and silence the world to the whisper of the leaves brushing against the telephone wire somewhere out there, where the black birds' claws wait for prancing prayers.

And then the sounds all swell in an awful crescendo. The murmuring soldiers' voices build and layer into harsh commands as they draw closer. The steady clang of metal buckles arranges into a pulsing deep heavy rhythm. It all crashes into your ears as the final approach nears. Any moment now, a knock on the door, and the question you know is coming, "Are any enemies of the regime in this dwelling?"

The thought hangs heavily in the air between you and the door. You brace yourself, fingers pressing the smooth lip of the bowl as though grounding yourself in something inanimate and physical might help.

And then, the knock. Clear and close.

You are a good person and it's time to make a decision to tell a lie or not.

Frameworks at War

When I served as a judge for the National High School Ethics Bowl in New York City, I was privileged to have a front-row seat to some intriguing moral debates. The competition resembles a debate club but with some important differences.

Rather than being pegged to defending a certain side of an argument, students are tasked with analyzing moral scenarios, both fictional and real, before a panel of judges who evaluate the depth, skill, and consideration of ethical complexity which they display during the presentation and question-and-answer portions. Since the students aren't assigned positions, I've seen teams "win" while changing their minds mid-discussion, revisiting the scenario with new perspectives raised by their "opponents." In this way, the Ethics Bowl has a remarkable openness that allows students to explore ethical reasoning in ways that conventional adversarial debates do not.

I absolutely encourage you to get involved with the program as a judge, coach, or participant. Or, at the very least, to check out the deep archive of cases online. The scenarios are an excellent way to spark lively discussions on a date night (warning: certain hot-button cases may lead to cancellation of the next date).

The Khmer Rouge scenario that I just put us through was not one of the cases, but the underlying "moral dilemma" it surfaces is present in nearly every one that I came across. In simple terms, you are faced with pondering the morality of telling the truth. It's presumed that you think that telling lies is generally a bad thing. In our scenario, the natural objection is that if you do lie (and the lie is believed) you are saving the lives of three humans, maybe four if you include yourself. That result far *outweighs* the moral violation of simply telling a lie. Especially telling a lie to someone like a Khmer Rouge soldier in 1976.

This situation pits two moral frameworks against each other. One is called **deontology**, the other is **consequentialism**. Deontology contends that there are moral rules which cannot be violated, and these are the rules by which we should evaluate the morality of an action. Consequentialism, on the other hand, contends that the morality of an action is evaluated based on the consequences of making or abstaining from the action. In simple terms, the deontologist says, "lying is always wrong," and the consequentialist responds with, "the morality of the action depends on the outcome."

If you are horrified by the deontologist's advice to our choice at the door in Cambodia, you are not alone. Most people find the position to be outrageous in its absolute adherence form. And this recoil leads nearly everyone to default to the other school of consequentialism.

Here's another standard case from the High School Ethics Bowl archives in which you can easily find this perennial framework clash:

> *A young black actor is struggling in Hollywood to land any big roles. He's low on money and barely scrapes by with small gigs for years on end. Then he gets his big chance and is offered a prominent role on a new sitcom loaded with huge stars and funded with a massive budget on a popular network. It's sure to be a big hit. He's overjoyed.*
>
> *The problem is that when he receives the script for the first season, he can't shake the feeling that the role that he is meant to portray is written in a way that is a harmful characterization of black culture. This portrayal clashes deeply with his ideas of positive depictions of minorities. He's quite certain that if he raises these concerns to the producers he will simply be replaced by another eager actor and dismissed.*

The consequentialist gets to work analyzing the moral decision. They might argue that if he *doesn't* take the role, he will have even more financial difficulty personally, and besides, if he is interested in being a role model and influencing societal change, the fame and attention he might get from the success of the show is necessary. Perhaps he could even donate some of his salary to causes he believes in. Or he could encourage the writers to adjust the character in future seasons after he has more bargaining power as a primary actor in the series. I mean, if he turns it down, they're just going to get another actor to take it who might not even care about positive future change. (You can probably sense that this is our Repairman beginning to tinker with the gears here. He has a whole consequentialism toolbox to use.)

The consequentialist could argue the other side of the ledger as well and consider that the societal harm done by the promotion of a racist stereotype "outweighs" any potential positive change or benefit he could enact by taking the role. Or that the personal consequences for his psyche might be too devastating, and he wouldn't be able to live with himself and therefore not make the positive change he is hoping to generate.

I can't help but think of several actors, actresses, or performers who use their platforms for advocating social causes *now* but partially built the foundations of those platforms by taking roles as cheap sex symbols or stereotyped clownish figures. Would Jane Fonda be able to rally for women's rights so effectively if she hadn't starred as the vapid sex-object lead in the smash hit *Barbarella* in 1968?

The deontologist would be unmoved by *any* of the consequentialist arguments, and rather focus on what kind of rule should govern the behavior of this actor. Perhaps, declining the role regardless of the fame and opportunity for change it might bring because "racism is always wrong." Or our deontologist could adopt a rule of deferring to the free market and chasing wealth, and take the role based on that rule-based commitment.

During a more recent real-life pop-culture media spectacle, the publicly broadcast lawsuit between actors Johnny Depp and Amber Heard, a series of uncomfortable and vulnerable audio recordings were played for both the courtroom and the online crowd of popcorn-munching commenters. In one of these recordings, the two ex-lovers try to pull each other down from some imagined moral high ground by mocking the kinds of roles the other took early in their career. Each tries to frame the other's success as the result of "selling out", taking shallow, sexist roles as empty sex objects.

Amber mocks Johnny for his work on *21 Jump Street,* saying it was those kinds of roles that helped him gain the fame he now uses to donate to charities and support so-called good causes. Johnny responds by accusing a younger Amber of doing the exact same thing, taking pathetic, hypersexualized parts instead of being a serious actress.

What they're really doing is accusing each other of having a consequentialist moral framework, while each merely pretends to operate from a more "honorable" deontological one. It sounded something like this:

"It's always wrong to take a sexist role!" (A deontological claim.)

"You did it too!"

"Yes, but I had to. It helped me get famous, and now I use that fame for good!" (A consequentialist line of argumentation.)

"Hypocrite!"

Moral philosophy is sometimes disguised in a chemically enhanced lovers' spat, and it almost always works like those parentheticals.

In another classic scenario I once judged, a fire breaks out in the Louvre, and someone is lying unconscious next to the *Mona Lisa*. You only have time to save one. Which do you save?

The deontologist might argue that preserving human life is an absolute duty, while the consequentialist could argue that rescuing the *Mona Lisa,* an irreplaceable artifact of immense cultural value, could actually benefit more people in the long run by preserving a piece of humanity's shared heritage. Visitors to the *Mona Lisa* are enchanted and inspired. The tourism money generated by Paris can be funneled to lifesaving social programs. We have to factor all of that and weigh it against the life of this one lady. Don't we?

Or perhaps you played the consequentialist and deontological cards in the opposite manner in the *Mona Lisa* case where we would need to know what type of person that lady was and weigh her future benefit to society against the *Mona Lisa*'s? Maybe she is an awful bigot about to murder people? Maybe you have a deontological rule about the sacred value of cultural artifacts.

This ability to play consequentialism and deontology on both sides of *every* argument hints at the deeper problems with this entire way of thinking.

The Realism Rift and the Grounding Problem

Underneath these "frameworks" is a much deeper split in moral philosophy, stretching beyond questions of rules and outcomes, and reaching into questions about the fundamental nature of morality. At the deepest levels, we arrive at a philosophical chasm that separates "moral objectivism" from "moral subjectivism." This split can be thought of as the difference between *discovering* and *inventing* moral truths. Moral objectivism, or moral realism, holds that moral facts exist independently of human beliefs or perceptions, akin to the way we might *discover* mathematical truths. Just as numbers and equations feel "found" rather than "invented," moral realism suggests that right and wrong are woven into the very fabric of the universe, waiting to be uncovered.

This deepest split in the conversation between moral realists and their opponents leads to an endless constellation of moral frameworks and philosophical suggestions. Of the exhaustive world of "isms and ists" that you would encounter in academic seminars, I am, perhaps unfairly, reducing the entire syllabus to the generally representative ideas of "consequentialism" and "deontology." But, to give you a taste of what someone who has spent far too many nights studying the field might throw at you, here is a brief look down each side of the chasm.

Under moral realism, we find concepts like divine command theory, natural law, and objective goodness. Divine command theory holds that moral facts stem directly from the will of a higher power, an idea with roots in various religious traditions. Natural law proposes that ethical principles are inherent to human nature and discernible through reason, independent of divine influence.

Some versions of utilitarianism (which falls under the consequentialist frameworks and seeks to make decisions which "maximize flourishing" and "minimize suffering") can fall under the auspices of moral realism. One can treat the maxim of generating the "greatest good for the greatest number" as an objective moral fact.

This particular form of non-divine and secular moral realism has seen a fervent resurgence in recent centuries. Most recently, it has gained some interesting support under the banner of "effective altruism."

I'll have some more to say about these potentially noble, potentially psychologically vulnerable, efforts, but for our moral philosophy introductory purposes in this chapter, just notice that whether you're invoking an ancient divine text, objective logical reasoning, or the supposed mathematically measurable well-being of sentient beings, *moral realism* grounds itself in the belief that morality is objective, timeless, and universal. This does not necessarily mean it is discoverable. There are moral realist theories that posit that moral truths are out there but not discoverable or comprehensible by man, only God. This sounds plausible enough, but it eats its own tail pretty quickly by presenting a discoverable moral fact about undiscoverable moral facts while also describing a pretty strange and vindictive God who creates a board game of existence but writes the rule book in a language you could never decipher.

On the other hand, moral anti-realism or moral subjectivism sees morality as a human creation, a framework of ethical "rules" that societies invent rather than discover. It rejects the idea that there could be some "godly view from nowhere" vantage-point from which one could definitely evaluate the morality of any action.

Within the moral anti-realism view, frameworks like nihilism, moral constructivism, and virtue ethics fall.

Moral anti-realism accepts that there's no "correct" moral answer independent of human perception and choice, rather, right and wrong are social constructions. Some anti-realists lean into cultural relativism, arguing that morality is entirely context-dependent and cannot be universalized across time and space. Moral anti-realism suggests that ethical values are, at least partially, products of the human experience, cultural conditioning, or individual perspective.

What I'm dancing around here is referred to as "the grounding problem" in moral philosophy, which presents the challenge of trying to trace one's moral ideas to some kind of solid objective or nonhuman foundation.

We can easily recognize the psychological appeal of this kind of thing. The Repairman is a huge fan of finding ground that you did not create. If you find the gears in your mind clashing and wondering if you are a good person, it is a kind of sweet relief to appeal to a grounding not of your own making or responsibility which ended up dictating the action you took. This sounds like a religious habit, doesn't it? And certainly there are religious minds who appeal to this relief by adhering to biblical rules, or divine revelation, to dictate or explain their own behavior. But don't make the mistake of limiting this psychological crutch to the religious. The appeal of ethical rules which are grounded in something outside of oneself is universal, and potentially much *more* common to find in purely supposedly secular political tribes and authoritarian psychologies.

I'll have much more to say about this powerful Repairman tool of helping us submit to one of many "moral grounding solutions" in later chapters. But what I want you to notice at this point is how neither consequentialism nor deontology *escape* the grounding problem. Either the rules of deontology are invented or discovered, or the moral measurements of certain outcomes are invented or discovered. The tortuous ultimate question of moral objectivity is not so easily resolved.

The Moral Clarity of the Unemployed

As a judge, watching students grapple with these two competing frameworks, it was hard not to question how much the philosophical foundations actually *help* us in making real world decisions.

I recall students deliberating the case about the black actor. Both teams in that case argued passionately that the actor should *reject* the role. Mostly, they did this by using deontological appeals to a kind of sacred rule against promoting racism.

They sharply tore into the poison of discriminatory racial power balances. There wasn't much deliberation of the consequences if the young man had taken the role and become quite famous and started a charity or anything like that. It was simply a presentation about the deep evil of racism. End of argumentation.

I don't recall which school argued a nearly identical position more skillfully, but at the lunch break I spoke to just about every participating school who seemed to all share the same view. As anecdotal evidence, I find that high schoolers (at least in America) are very attracted to moral realism of the deontological type with an emphasis of "duties" and "societal roles." Perhaps, this is because of the constant injection of a hierarchical, nearly militaristic order and duty-bound roles in their otherwise chaotic and messy teenage lives.

It's not that I necessarily disagreed with their resulting position on the actor and his dilemma, but I couldn't help but wonder how all of these 16-year-olds in front of me might respond to this same dilemma a decade later as 26-year-olds. In that crucial post high school decade which awaits them, perhaps a few will be presented with a lucrative offer at a not-so-ethical law firm, tech start-up, or junk food corporation.

I can't help but wonder if the consequentialist framework and "logic" awaits them. This is what I call The Mundane Dilemma. It has become so ubiquitous in a capitalist society as to be barely recognizable as a problem anymore. Common expressions like "a conservative is just a liberal who was mugged by reality" should be popping up in your head at this point, or "one cannot be a moral purist, one has to be a realist," or "everyone has to eat, right?"

You could imagine dinner table conversations with one of these high school students. Her father, who just worked all day for a company or institution that his younger self would have been appalled by, asks his daughter what she thinks the actor should do. He hears her righteous argument that he should absolutely reject the offer and the money. After the father chokes down a forkful of his hard-earned meal, he might present a consequentialist counterargument about all the good he could do with the money and fame. Perhaps, the daughter looks around at the luxury house and wonders how much of that "potential good" her family is enacting.

This dinner could get quickly out of hand in our imaginations: a fight about her wanting to go to an expensive college, the father showing the donation he just gave to a charity to help the homeless, an argument about the car she is asking for and his suggestion that she go for a second-hand cheaper one. It could end with the father scoffing the whole thing off with, "just wait until you're my age with a mortgage and a bratty righteous teenager!"

I probably participated in a few arguments like this. Sorry, Dad.

These arguments have basically swallowed up the entire political landscape. They are awful. They are endless. They are a deontological position arguing against a consequentialist one on a seesaw of eternal bullshit accusations. But there *is* another way. I'll get us there by the end of this book.

How to Impress a Room and Still Miss the Point

After all, what good is the endless parsing of these terms if it doesn't lead us to any more clarity in the midst of a genuine ethical crisis? I've been around academic philosophers who can talk in circles with all the "isms" and jargons. It's like listening to someone assemble an intricate argument out of endlessly interchangeable Lego blocks. And it can sometimes feel like academic moral philosophy is more interested in categorizing every possible or conceivable framework than in providing tools for real-world application. Scholars chase the coining of a new "ism" with the same vigor that a politician might rebrand a recycled tax proposal hoping the public will consider it a brilliant revolutionary idea. It's as if moral philosophy has a fetish for precision that loses sight of its actual purpose. The result? A field that's more like a linguistic playground than a guide to ethical living.

Yet as I will argue in the following chapters, moral philosophy *does* offer us something of real value *only* when it is in direct conversation with psychology: the ability to self-identify and recognize the patterns we fall into as we resolve cognitive dissonance. If you're aware that you're leaning toward consequentialist reasoning to avoid guilt or invoking deontological principles to justify a difficult choice, you're already a step closer to understanding your motivations. Rather than serving as a final say on what is "right" and "wrong," these frameworks can act more like mirrors, showing us the mental gymnastics we engage in when caught in moral predicaments. And it doesn't matter how fancy and academically informed your "ism" sounds.

In fact, one of the most useful insights moral philosophy offers isn't a definitive answer but a realization that we're rarely consistent. People love to claim that they're deontologists or consequentialists as if these labels were solid ground. Yet, under pressure, we switch frameworks to suit our needs. One minute we're standing firmly against lying as a moral absolute, and the next, we're defending a "noble lie" that we believe is harmless or even helpful.

Knowing the difference between deontology and consequentialism, or realism and anti-realism, is valuable only to the extent that it helps us see ourselves more clearly. It lets us name the ways we wiggle out of discomfort, how we justify, how we excuse, how we struggle. That is not nothing, but it is *not* an answer in itself. Moral philosophy is a kind of roadmap for self-awareness and that is all we should ask of it.

And we should be wary of a certain appeal to naming ourselves with "isms" and "ists." Academic philosophy has long been plagued, and sometimes stalled, by these labels. They offer shortcuts, but they can also become crutches, allowing us to outsource our thinking. Used wisely, they're precise tools. But the moment they start thinking for us, we're no longer doing philosophy, we're dissolving into ideological acid.

The Hypocrisy Hustle: Moves and Motives

Now that you've got the basic framework of consequentialist versus deontological moral reasoning, you're going to start spotting it *everywhere*. Watch any news panel, political debate, or dinner table argument and it'll show up, usually fast. It might come wrapped in folksy charm, cloaked in moral outrage, or laced with technocratic language, but the structure is always the same: someone argues from principle, and someone else argues from outcome. And those someones are liable to flip on the next topic or the next election cycle.

You can learn to spot it in basic vocabulary. Words like "norms," "rights," "duty," "obligations," or "principle" usually signal a deontological stance. Whereas terms like "necessary," "effective," "realistic," or "pragmatic" are favorite tools of the consequentialist.

Take free speech, for example. A self-proclaimed defender of free speech might insist that all viewpoints must be protected, no matter how offensive. That's a deontological argument. "Speech is a sacred principle, period." But when protesters chant "Free Palestine" or criticize police brutality, that same defender may suddenly worry about "national security," "community safety," or "appropriateness," which are all consequentialist concerns. The principle shifts depending on whose voice is speaking or the potential consequences of the speech.

Or consider the abortion debate, where appeals to the "sanctity of life" are often used to argue against a woman's right to choose. That sounds like a deontological position: life is sacred, no exceptions. But the same individual may support the death penalty or morally permit abortion in cases of rape or incest, or shrug off the deaths of civilians in foreign wars as "necessary collateral damage." Suddenly, the sacredness of life becomes situational based on the outcome.

Whenever politicians talk about "red lines," they are talking about deontological lines. Whenever those lines are inevitably crossed and suddenly there are new considerations which make this politician draw "new red lines" they have been revealed to be consequentialists.

Think, too, of the famous case of dropping an atomic bomb on Hiroshima. One side says the deliberate bombing of civilians is inherently immoral, full stop. That's the deontologist speaking. The other says it was tragic but necessary to end the war and save more lives; that's the consequentialist. Recently, the eye-popping phrases "escalate to deescalate" or "peace through force" encapsulate this flexible logic. Two entirely different moral languages can clash over the same historical event.

Sometimes the hypocrisy debate is not disguised at all, as was the case when Joe Biden, after years of insisting on upholding the "norms" of respecting the justice system and the "principles" which undergird the nation and the "sanctity" of the jury process in America, pardoned his son Hunter Biden in the final month of his presidency. Many in the media, both liberal and right leaning outlets, were quick to pounce on this "hypocrisy." The defense of Biden's sudden switch could only be hashed out in consequentialist terms by pointing out that Trump's campaign promises of retribution and vengeance on his political enemies had changed the landscape of moral considerations. Fine. But what was the point, then, of promoting and declaring adherence to "principles" which are fundamentally steadfast and immune to consequences? (You can now impress your friends by explaining as a "moral philosopher" that this was a jump from deontology to consequentialism.)

Accusations of hypocrisy inevitably follow, as the initial stance based on an absolute principle becomes situationally flexible.

The Sacred Snap

A critical question: can two principles, both considered sacred, be invoked in direct opposition to each other? Take "sovereignty" and "self-defense."

Can sovereignty, upheld as inviolable, be disregarded in the name of self-defense? And when this happens, are we not simply watching as deontologists conveniently collapse into consequentialists, willing to compromise on principle if the situation feels compelling enough? It's as if the principles themselves can only be counted on up to a certain threshold of inconvenience or emotional investment, after which they seem to *snap* into something else.

This tension introduces a common critique I'll be exploring throughout this book: the potentially infinite elasticity of consequentialism. If we are willing to abandon a principle when the stakes become high enough, are we ultimately committing to any principle at all? Can anything be justified if we stretch the consequentialist rationale far enough, so long as we assert the right outcomes? By raising the stakes high enough, whether with appeals to security, survival, or the "greater good," the initial principle (whether it be free speech, the sanctity of life, or the sovereignty of territory) seems to lose its foothold, crumbling under the profound weight of desired outcomes.

But this isn't just about calling people hypocrites. That's the easy part. And it's kind of fun, admittedly. The real work is understanding why this toggling happens, and how we might learn to engage with it more honestly. Because these shifts don't always come from bad faith. They come from fear, confusion, and the sheer messiness of living in a world where the clean lines of principle and the sharp math of consequence rarely align.

Though, I do know that some people are absolutely operating out of bad faith. Those are the hypocritical jerks. And we all know plenty of them. See? Feels kind of good, doesn't it?

Neoliberalism and the Ethics of Spending Yourself

Consequentialism has become so baked into our assumed existential orientations, that even common comparative words and phrases like something being "worth it," or "beneficial" are a subtle nod to a utilitarian type of moral-mathematics. Sometimes it can be as simple as invoking the word "spend," as in "spending energy on a problem" which implies a utilitarian zero-sum game of resources of moral attention.

This kind of deep, almost invisible reliance on consequentialist logic has become so natural that we barely notice it. More and more thinkers have started calling this bleed of market-style reasoning into every corner of life "neoliberalism."

Now, *neoliberalism* is a notoriously slippery word, one that seems to mutate daily depending on who's using it. I've had discussions with free-market libertarians, social-democrats, and neo-conservatives whose eyes all rolled to the back of their heads upon hearing the word brought up in casual critical conversation. I think neoliberalism is a fine word for what philosophers like George Monbiot have referenced as *The Invisible Doctrine,* or documentary filmmakers like Adam Curtis seem to describe in his free-wheeling documentaries like *Can't Get You Out of My Head.*

Here is the way I understand it. It's nearly identical to what sociologist Erich Fromm described in his 1955 book *The Sane Society* as the "marketing orientation." Fromm argued that in modern capitalist societies, people begin to see themselves as commodities, valued not for who they are, but for how well they can package and sell themselves. Life becomes one long cost-benefit analysis, where even our existential identities are subject to market logic. How desirable are we? How much are we worth? How "investable"?

The political theorist Wendy Brown, drawing on the work of French philosopher Michel Foucault, describes how neoliberal rationality has extended far beyond markets. In her view, individuals are recast as *homo economicus,* entrepreneurial actors expected to treat every domain of life as an opportunity for self-investment and value enhancement. Education becomes a way to build human capital. Dating becomes a strategy for maximizing compatibility returns. It is a transformation in how we think, reason, and relate to ourselves and each other.

I think this mindset has been reinforced by the rise of "citizen capitalism," where platforms like Airbnb and Uber draw ordinary people into direct participation in market logic. The naturalness by which we begin to see others less as neighbors and more as potential customers, competitors, or assets to manage is alarming.

Whatever we call it, in moral terms the market doesn't just determine who wins or loses in an amoral system confined to economic activity and patterns, it becomes the arbiter of what is *right* or *wrong, true* or *false*. The "marketplace" becomes the acid test of all values. We can see how this logic can pass for a kind of secular liberation, and has become the rallying cry of many market-loving libertarians around the world. But it also raises the troubling possibility that we haven't liberated ourselves from divine judgment so much as outsourced it to our unexamined impulses.

Neoliberalism also carries with it the notion of globalization which goes beyond the obvious interconnected forms of global trade and currency intertwining. The neoliberal mentality (and I do think it is fair to call it that) becomes a self-evident and self-assured position that this really is the only way to organize not just a society, but a moral life as well.

That all might sound a bit abstract or overly academic, but I think it's a crucial insight and one that I will continue to unfold in more detail in following chapters. In fact, as the title of this book suggests, I believe the entirety of market-logic becomes fatally flawed when the price of admission is paid with our moral integrity on a market full of products of increasingly obvious hollow spiritual value.

I would bet that, even before the full argument is laid out, many readers will already grok what I'm pointing to. There's an intuitive discomfort that bubbles up when we stretch consequentialist logic too far, especially when we start applying it to our deepest moral instincts. But the real challenge is recognizing that discomfort *without* immediately defaulting to the assumed other path and clinging to deontology as if it's the *only* alternative. I've seen this move in some thoughtful commentators who, upon admitting defeat to the inadequacy of the secular utilitarian path, end up turning, oftentimes *re*turning, to deontological religious moral doctrines. But those frameworks suffer from the very same kind of hollowness. They can't escape the same core grounding question of morality.

There is another way.

Moral Fatigue: Rules, Results, Retreat, and Wanting to Be a Bird

By now, you've probably noticed the trap. Maybe you've even felt it.

You're pulled between people demanding rigid moral principles and others offering endlessly flexible, context-sensitive trade-offs. And you? You just want to make lunch and maybe not feel like a monster for buying the wrong kind of almond milk (didn't you know that it is a *really* water intensive process?!). Welcome to moral fatigue.

At some point, most people try to escape the bind altogether. If morality only comes in two flavors, rules or results, eventually you get tired of chewing. Which brings us to the third "r," retreat.

This is the path of opting out, of mentally exiting the swirling contradictions, and building a private sanctuary where moral demands feel distant. It's understandable. It might even feel necessary. Maybe you've already built your version of this — some combination of turning off the news, curating your feed, or watching debates like a nature documentary. Look at them go.

I always think of a famous scene in a movie that I actually don't like very much called *A Few Good Men*, where Jack Nicholson's character, Colonel Jessep, is being grilled by Tom Cruise's Lieutenant Kaffee in a courtroom. The case is about some pretty ugly, maybe illegal, definitely f-ed up stuff that Jessep's military unit was doing. Kaffee is demanding the truth.

And after a few tense moments of evasion, Jessep explosively yells, "You can't handle the truth! Son, we live in a world that has walls, and those walls have to be guarded by men with guns. Who's gonna do it? You? You, Lt. Weinberg? I have a greater responsibility than you could possibly fathom. You weep for Santiago and you curse the Marines. You have that luxury. You have the luxury of not knowing what I know — that Santiago's death, while tragic, probably saved lives. And my existence, while grotesque and incomprehensible to you, saves lives. You don't want the truth because deep down in places you don't talk about at parties, you want me on that wall — you need me on that wall!"

And you know what? I know plenty of people who basically nod at that point and say, "You know what? He's right. I don't want to know. I can't handle it. Don't tell me about all the awful stuff you do in order for me to enjoy my bottle of Snapple at this party."

But this retreat can still take on a haunting form of engagement. In our era, this appears as what philosopher Slavoj Žižek terms "pseudo-activity." Rather than fully opting out, we keep one foot in by voting or promoting candidates who themselves grapple with the very moral conflicts from which we've withdrawn. In this way, we act through a representative, someone who is willing to confront the decisions we hesitate to make ourselves.

Because the line from Colonel Jessep is more than a line defending military secrecy; it speaks to the unspoken contract many of us make with our leaders. "You don't have the courage to pull the lever on the trolley problems of the world and face the wreckage. You can't shoot a rocket into the bedroom when the bad guy is reading his daughter a story. But I'll do it for you. Vote for me!" And so, we gladly do. In electing others to make these moral decisions, we get the comfort of "participation" without confronting the true weight of the choices. So, it's understandable that you might want to step back, to look away, and to feel exhaustion.

I've also heard the retreat impulse, and frankly felt it many times, in an existential way. It comes as a longing to no longer be burdened with this awful condition of being a *human*. I have a friend who often looks at the birds and really envies them. He wants to be one, wants to escape into those lives. I mean, the flying part looks pretty cool, I'll admit, but what he is really longing for is what he thinks is the "freedom" of the birds. To not have responsibility. To not be concerned with a national border or complex moral considerations. To not have to write your own agenda. A bird knows what the task of the day, the hour, or the second is. And she does not question it. She doesn't even have the mind to do so. She does not know that she can wonder about what it would be like to be a human. I think we've all felt this desire, though we may pick different animals.

But being a bird is not moral freedom. It is the absence of it.

The bird certainly has valence and consciousness and choices to make, yes. The bird has desires. It has emotions and an inner life. It has *wants*. Those are called first-order desires. But what it doesn't have is second-order desires. It doesn't ask the question, what do I *want* to *want*? Or what ought I desire? What kind of bird ought I be? Or should I want to be human?

Those are the types of questions which torture us humans. And from that torture springs art, morality, and much despair and confusion.

I understand the desire to deny it, or hand it back over to whatever diabolical creator granted us such a maddening ability to wonder. I'll be devoting more time to this terribly heavy freedom as we push further into the existential chapters. But for now, I have a plea.

Don't go.

Don't slide back into your cocoon just yet. Don't scroll away into a haze of takes and side quests. I know the options on the table — rules, results, retreat — can feel like the full set. But I promise you, there's something else. Something more interesting, more human, and more honest.

We'll get there. Just keep reading. I won't let you off the hook that easily, little birdie.

You Now Hold the Instruments of Interruption

So now you're holding both instruments, the strange flashlight that lets you spot the Cognitive Dissonance Repairman. You now know how to look out for the moment when a belief changes not because of new information, but because the tension of holding two contradictory thoughts became too uncomfortable. You know the feeling. That's the Repairman at work. We'll continue to call out his unwanted tricks.

The second tool isn't so much a light as it is a warped and twitchy moral scale. It's the instrument that lights up when it hears the oh-so-tiring performance of people pitting "principle" against "consequence," "means" against "ends," "values" against "outcomes," over and over in new costumes. It's what gives us the illusion that hypocrisy is a decisive moral failure rather than just an unexamined moral position, which might be the same thing in the end.

Both of these instruments are essential for what comes next. Think of them like little alarm systems with blinking warning lights. Symptom detectors which make a fuss when they sense some lazy, weak, or bad moral thinking.

As we move forward, we're not just going to watch people (including yours truly) rationalize, or accuse each other of hypocrisy, or endlessly trade barbs in moral debates, we're going to try to understand the deeper emotional and philosophical terrain underneath all that. So, take your tools. Keep them close. And hop back in the time machine. We're going to be assessing our loudly cracking world.

Chapter 4

Nervous Statues

Our age of reckoning

A Forecast for Unraveling

This chapter is the hinge of the book. If Chapters 1 and 2 scratched the surface on a philosophical dissection of what "history" might mean, and Chapter 3 threw the psychological wrench of cognitive dissonance into the maddening contradictions of default modern moral reasoning, then Chapter 4 is where those ideas converge around a single burning question: Why all the upheaval now?

We're living through a strange split. On one side is a simmering revolution, where statues fall and myths crumble, and the Global South speaks with new confidence. On the other side is a kind of moral retreat, a weary stillness that feels like being trapped in a machine that once promised progress but now just grinds on without purpose. That tension is the emotional core of this book. I've called it the zone of insufficient reward. It's where systems still demand our belief, our labor, and our moral loyalty, but offer only contradiction and disappointment in return. Some people sit with that tension and rationalize it. Others break through it and start pushing.

This is the fracture beneath our moment — this growing sense that history is being rewritten, not just in books or museums, but inside each of us. So, why this global moment of reckoning? Why is moral clarity suddenly so urgent and so elusive?

I'll explore five overlapping explanations to this question in Chapter 5. They aren't mutually exclusive, and you don't have to pick a favorite. Some are hopeful, others unsettling. Each offers a lens on the turbulence. But one of them is not like the others, and it's the most powerful and incendiary of them all.

But before we get to those, let's focus our mental cameras in this chapter on something immediate. A statue sinking into Bristol Harbor will do nicely.

The Moral Material of Stone and Story

In the past decade, more than 300 statues have been removed across the Global North. Just some of the names include:

Christopher Columbus, Robert E. Lee, Jefferson Davis, Charles Darwin, George Washington, Don Juan de Oñate, Philip Schuyler, Thomas Jefferson, Theodore Roosevelt, Cecil Rhodes, Edward Colston, Henry Dundas, Winston Churchill, Victor Schœlcher, and Indro Montanelli. Most removals followed public outcry from vocal, if not always large, groups of citizens. Others were carried out preemptively by local councils, wary of unrest or headlines. This particular form of protest against statues and building names has recently morphed into fights over the names of bodies of water like the Gulf of Mexico/America, or the Persian/Arabian Gulf.

I'm really not going to give you a direct argument for or against statue removal. And I'm not here to provide a defense or condemnation of the men they commemorate. And yes, it's nearly all men. There *have been* some controversies over statues depicting women, though, interestingly these statues are symbolic representations, rather than depictions of specific historical figures. For example, the "Comfort Women" statues across Asia are a reference to the girls forced into sexual slavery by the Japanese military during WWII. These statues, showing barefoot young women beside empty chairs, have sparked repeated diplomatic protests from Japan.

But this book *isn't* about statues. It's concerned with what statues represent, the way our historical narratives buttress our present-day moral reasoning, and the complications of judging historical figures and epochs. Let's see if we can apply our new tools of inquiry and chisel out an entirely new space to reconsider how we talk about morality and if *we* can adequately judge a man like Edward Colston or the period in which the statue was commissioned, and what the relationship between those judgments may be.

The Edward Colston case is a story that is more than a biographical study, it's a prism. Through it, we can examine four distinct moral flashpoints: the height of his wealth generation in the late 1600s as a cog of the British slave trade; his funeral in 1721, where he was mourned as a local benefactor; the Victorian era of 1895, when Bristol's elite raised a statue in his honor long after slavery had been abolished; and the moment in 2020 when protesters tore that statue down and threw it into the harbor.

Each moment reflects a distinct configuration of moral reasoning, collective memory, and cognitive dissonance. But we can use the same tools to examine all of them. Together, they offer a handy representative timeline of how societies and individuals rationalize, sanctify, and eventually confront the violence they've built into their foundations. Even if those foundations support an impressive amount of technological comfort.

Do Hollow Statues Float?

Edward Colston lived in the latter half of the 17th century and made his fortune in the Royal African Company (RAC), which held a monopoly on the English slave trade. At its height, the company operated over 46 ships, making it one of the largest players in the trade. A typical RAC ship would load up its human cargo at Cape Coast Castle on the Gold Coast (modern-day Ghana) along with gold, ivory, and other commodities. About 500 chained Africans would be ushered through the intentionally narrow "gate of no return" and crammed into inhumane underbelly conditions to begin their journey westward towards the Americas.

Edward Colston never personally saw any of this. He served as the primary shareholder and decision-maker while sitting in Bristol, England. If you picture the triangle voyage of a ship leaving England loaded with goods, headed for the West African coast to trade for new goods and humans, travel across the ocean to trade those goods and humans, and head back to England with profit and new goods, the England vantage point of the triangle never has to "dirty its hands" with African slaves.

For his part, Colston, who never married, funneled a good portion of his wealth into charitable causes. He established schools serving disadvantaged families, supported almshouses that cared for the elderly poor, provided free shelter for sailors on his merchant ships, donated to hospitals, and created large endowments for the church. He was widely celebrated for all of this "good will." But, suffice it to say, Edward Colston did not participate in my brave boycott from Chapter 1. In fact, his company would top any contemporary "do-not-buy-from" list.

RAC ceased operations in 1752, when its charter expired and the British government weakened its monopoly to allow more decentralized competition, but not before it had participated in the forced enslavement and transportation of tens of thousands of West Africans to the Americas while generating huge amounts of wealth for England. Estimates indicate an average profit margin of 38% per voyage with annual revenues around £300,000. This translates, with inflation adjustments, to the equivalent of £102,700,000 in total profits over Colston's 12-year involvement with the company. At a time when the global economy was much smaller, and wealth much more concentrated in a few empires, this "market share" might be equivalent to a global brand like Coca-Cola today.

He died on October 11, 1721, at his residence in Mortlake, Surrey. His funeral was a spectacle. His body was transported to Bristol, where he was interred at All Saints' Church. He arranged in his will for the procession to feature children and poor residents of his almshouses as pallbearers. They sang psalms and wore new clothes he had provided in his final donations. The whole affair reads as a fascinating form of psychological moral shielding for his legacy.

In Colston's England, popular attitudes toward the slave trade were just beginning to shift in the final decade of his life. Colston himself did not leave many quotes or passages of writing about his stance on slavery but common arguments from his time were made by people like James Tobin. Those sounded like this, "The ignorance and barbarism in which the African tribes exist renders them incapable of any regular society; their lives are a perpetual scene of bloodshed, superstition, and licentiousness." He insisted that slavery introduced them to Christianity and discipline, thus benefiting them morally.

Popular moral philosophers like John Locke, viewed as an important Enlightenment thinker and sometimes credited as the "father of liberalism" for his ideas about "the social contract," personally invested in the Royal African Company. Locke also helped draft the Fundamental Constitutions of Carolina, which gave explicit protections to slaveholders, including provisions allowing "absolute power and authority" over enslaved people.

Colston's company took this "absolute power" notion to a grotesque end. It literally branded the letters RAC on the chest, back, or shoulders of its slaves with hot irons. This branding was usually done just before embarking on the middle passage. The hot iron brand would mark children as young as 4 or 5 years old. This practice was not unique to the RAC.

It would take another fifty years for landmark legal cases such as *Somerset v. Stewart* (1772) to begin whittling away at the practice's legal foundations, ultimately leading to its abolition throughout the British Empire in 1833.

"Few Rise Superior"

Fast forward 187 years to June 7, 2020. Cheering protesters pull Colston's statue from its perch, spray-paint its face, jump on its head and torso, and throw it into Bristol Harbor. The symbolic act of dumping the Colston-shaped bronze into the water carries with it a heavy dose of poetic justice, especially when one recalls the hundreds of thousands of African captives who died during the Middle Passage and whose bodies were tossed into the Atlantic.

Protesters gathered at Colston's now-empty plinth in the middle of a boulevard. Speakers climbed up to where the statue once stood, delivering impassioned pleas. One woman shouted, "It's time to take a stand together and fight this racist system! Think about your children! Don't turn the other cheek. Don't say it has nothing to do with me. We can change things!"

The city fished the statue out of the harbor, draped it in a blue plastic sheet, and escorted it by motorboat while a smattering of protesters jeered. A far cry from Colston's self-designed funeral parade through weeping streets a hundred years prior. The statue now lies in a museum, displayed on its back with graffiti still preserved on its face and legs. It's situated at knee level, an intentional reversal of its former high point.

So, how are we to think of the morality of Edward Colston himself? Do our tools of moral analysis help us at all? Can we apply the deontological versus consequentialist lens? Can we enter Colston's head to appreciate the cognitive dissonance he may have felt, if any at all, when donating his slave-boosted wealth to the Bristol needy? Can we surmise the ways in which his internal Repairman may have allowed him to look in the mirror and even know he might one day be the subject of a statue in his town? Can we be so sure that we would have behaved differently at any stage of his life?

2020 wasn't the first time Bristolians had questioned the lionizing of Colston. Writing in 1920, a local author named H.J. Wilkins compiled an account of Colston's life and works, detailing his accumulation of wealth and his charitable endeavors. Wilkins, while clearly defending Colston's legacy, made a pitch for the complexities of moral judgment. Referring to the "character" of Edward Colston with an acknowledgement of the slavery he facilitated, he wrote, "Edward Colston, then, was the product of an intolerant age, tolerance, as now understood, being unknown at this period. But few rise superior to their own times."

That final line is so striking. And so damning.

Is not morality a measure of how well one can "rise superior" to their own times? Is morality actually a measure of how well one can resist the lure of conformity or justificationism when one becomes aware of the immorality of the crowd? If we are merely "products of an age" can we claim to be independent responsible moral agents at all?

But let's slow our indignation for Colston down a bit, no matter how difficult that is. Let's remember, of course, that Colston had a Cognitive Dissonance Repairman tinkering away in his head. I would venture that his Repairman was *very* hard at work with getting his "I'm a good person" gear to spin in the right direction. All of that charity engagement was real. Was it not? All the Christianity that he was digesting was too. The utilitarian tool was patching things up, or attempting to, with appeals to the "greater good" and the economic *necessity* of wealth generation and his efforts to redistribute it to the impoverished. The dehumanization tool was sealing cracks too. The arguments about "lesser creatures" being "better off" under enslavement, being made by prominent philosophers and religious leaders, were surely at work in his mind.

None of these may be decisive winning arguments for a less harsh moral judgment of a man like Edward Colston. You may not let him off the hook. I certainly don't. But we must remember these as we move forward. Because the nature of these justifications are going to start sounding very familiar when we start applying them to other potential moral infractions that we all participate in.

Perhaps our infractions are not as "heavy" as human enslavement nor as "light" as fibbing to a student about turning wooden pegs, but that factor of the argument about the relative "moral weight of the infraction" will be unmasked and be understood as one of the most powerful Repairman tools, a tool which we must not underestimate.

An Unwitting Bodyguard and "Honoring the Empire" in Black Face

It's pertinent to know that Colston's statue was not erected during his lifetime (the lifetime that did not *know* tolerance, apparently) nor was it built in the immediate afterglow of his celebrated funeral in the 1720s. It was built 170 years later in 1895.

I find when writing, and reading, history, numbers like 170 can get kind of blurry. I have to frequently pause and put these things into human time-scale context. For instance, 170 years ago, photography was a brand-new invention and women couldn't vote almost anywhere on Earth. If I die tomorrow, I can barely imagine a world 170 years later when a statue, or hologram or whatever, might be built in my honor. The chances are quite low for me. But the weirdness holds even if you think of any business mogul, philanthropist, or political leader today.

In any case, 1895 was the height of the Victorian period, a time marked by extreme class stratification in a post-slavery British Empire. But it was a time when colonialism remained broadly celebrated, and attitudes in England still embraced the "civilizing mission" narrative to justify domination over "less civilized" parts of the world. This particular argumentation might sound familiar to you. It has been making a recent comeback with certain conservative commentators who more openly defend forms of Neo-Colonialism in defense of the American Empire and the legacy of European dominance.

The Edward Colston statue was the brainchild of a man named James Arrowsmith, who raised public funds to pay for it. We don't know much about Arrowsmith, but if we view him, as Wilkins suggests, as a "product of his (Victorian) age" we can imagine the motivations.

To try to get into contact with his historical *moral* moment, let's take a quick jaunt in the time machine. Head in there and I'll pull the lever. You might feel weird about this one.

~~~

It's May 24th, 1907. School is out across England. It's Queen Victoria's birthday, after all. It's "Empire Day" and you've been preparing for the celebration all week. Your schoolmates are already gathered by the Colston statue which has been standing for 12 years now. You vaguely remember the unveiling ceremony when you were just a small child. Classmates warm up their singing voices with "Rule, Britannia" and "God Save the Queen" in its shadow.

You know a little about Edward Colston. Your teachers mention his generosity, the schools and almshouses which owe their existence to his benevolence. The slave trade aspect of his business? It comes up in passing, but it's brushed off as a practice that was no longer accepted. You have some conflicting ideas about it. You haven't fully formed the moral argument, but you're beginning to question just how much a man like Colston *should* be celebrated. You keep these thoughts to yourself as you stare at the black shoe polish tin you're using as a makeup compact. You were assigned to the "African Tribal Leaders" section of the procession along with several other boys and girls from the town.

At first, your friend John, who was assigned to march with the Canadian Mounties section, was jealous that you'd get to go hunting for a new animal skin to emulate the primitive loin cloth practices of the Ashanti tribe, but he grew to like the idea of wearing his father's oversized boots and red jacket. And besides, he thought the polish made his skin break out last year.

Other kids dress up as exotic Indian Maharajahs and Princesses, rugged Australian Bushrangers, or colorful Caribbean Islanders. Empire Day would be an elaborate spectacle of the reach of the Queen. It was difficult for you to imagine yourself as anything else, but on "Empire Day," it was impossible for
~~~

you not to feel pride in being British. All these distant subjects must be grateful for the grace of this relationship.

You finish blackening your face, check your homemade spear. You wonder, idly, if you'll ever go to Africa. John is already babbling about new ocean liners and stories from his uncle's trip to the Dublin Exhibition, "a floating city," he calls it. "Progress," he grins, "is moving faster than we can think."

The parade is a spectacle of families and fun and costumed stereotypes.

And when it ends and candy wrappers swirl in the wind, you and John collapse near Colston's feet. His boots ache. Your face feels stiff with dried polish. The sun dips behind the rooftops. The statue looms behind you, watching.

We don't know exactly what John Cassidy, the Irish sculptor of the Edward Colston statue, intended with the solemn pose he gave his subject. Colton is depicted kind of looking down, arms crossed, hand on chin. Some have speculated it was a nod to the internal tension Colston *must* have carried, the weight of blood money transmuted into charity. Maybe that's just wishful projection. Cassidy himself was silent on the matter, at least in the recorded history.

But let's set Cassidy aside. The real story isn't about him or even about Colston. The real story is about 1895, the year the statue was erected, and what function the people of Bristol, particularly its industrial elite, *needed* it to do.

That same year, Bristol introduced electric tram service, the first in the United Kingdom. A marvel of technological progress. Clean, fast, modern. It connected neighborhoods in new ways, made commutes easier, and symbolized the shimmering promises of industrial capitalism. The world, they were told, was moving forward. And they had the trams to prove it.

But progress always comes from somewhere (so goes the utilitarian logic). And in the case of Victorian England, it came directly out of the coal-choked lungs of factory workers, the bent backs of child laborers, and the global scaffolding of empire — an empire built on centuries of extraction, exploitation, and brutality. The elites of 1895 were savvy enough to know this, even if they never said it out loud. They weren't amnesiacs. They knew about the Royal African Company. They knew Colston's fortune was made from branding human beings with hot irons. They knew, at some level, that the electric tram and Colston were part of the same moral ecosystem of utilitarian mathematics.

And that knowledge created a moral problem.

Because by 1895, the practice of slavery was no longer tenable. At least not openly. The British Empire had abolished it decades earlier. The country liked to think of itself as more moral now. But the moral philosophy underpinning the system of wealth had not changed. And so, a new kind of moral shield was needed to reinterpret the horror and to repackage cruelty as legacy.

That's what Colston's statue was. Not a tribute, but a bronze bodyguard. A public monument to the supposed necessity of moral compromise of empire, dressed up as civic gratitude.

By placing Colston on a pedestal — literally and figuratively — the industrialists of Bristol weren't just honoring a man. They were defending a worldview. They were saying something like, "Yes, terrible things happened! But look what we've built. Look at the schools. Look at the hospitals. Look at the tram. And, sure, we elite industrialists might be cracking a few eggs over your heads at the factories to make the omelets of trams. But this Colston guy did even worse in a utilitarian game. And we understand his logic and charity, don't we?!" It was an appeal to the logic of trade-offs, the age-old defense of "collateral damage." The ends justify the means. Wealth requires sacrifice. History demands winners.

And if you squint just right at the statue, Colston became less a slave trader and more a metaphor for all of them, for anyone who ever turned blood into philanthropy and wanted to be thanked for being the one "on the wall" of society. The Victorian public didn't need to admire him. They just needed him to sympathize with his moral mathematics in a time of "lower technology" when slave labor could not be so easily replaced by coal powered machines. They needed Colston to hold the moral line. To keep the deeper question, "Is this system worth it?" from bubbling to the surface.

And, remarkably, for 125 years, it worked.

Until 2020, when the statue was ripped down. At that moment, the moral shield shattered. And the question it had been holding back, "What are we really standing on?" finally surged into public view.

And not to be overlooked, Colston's statue came down just two weeks after George Floyd was murdered by a white police officer's suffocating knee in Minneapolis. This murder was broadcast on everyone's phone and quickly disseminated globally in a way that would be unimaginable to Colston himself or the Victorian elites who commissioned his statue.

Which slams us right into the hard question of the next chapter: **Why now?**

Relevant to that question, and to update the ongoing moral saga of Colston and his statue:

Just ten days after it was toppled, an unknown vandal smashed and defaced the honorary headstone of an enslaved African man in the nearby St. Mary's churchyard. The headstone honored "Scipio Africanus" (almost certainly not his preferred name), who died in 1720 at the age of 18. Born into slavery, Scipio served as a household servant for an English aristocrat, Charles Howard, 7th Earl of Suffolk, a far cry from the conditions most enslaved Africans endured. The headstone was preserved as a historical landmark until the attack, during which someone scrawled on nearby flagstones: "NOW LOOK AT WHAT YOU MADE ME DO. STOP PROTESTING. PUT COLSTON'S STATUE BACK OR THINGS WILL REALLY HEAT UP."

While I can't perform a full psychoanalysis of the vandal, I'll extend some charity. It's possible this person actually does support the slave trade, but I'd guess they align more closely with Wilkins' sentiment. They likely knew little about Edward Colston, but they certainly knew what the statue symbolized. The vandal generally isn't a fan of anyone digging around in history and rocking the boat of the status quo. Similarly, I'd wager most anti-statue protesters could say little about Colston beyond knowing he was a slave trader. As I've said, this book isn't about statues, and statues aren't really about people.

To date, there have been numerous attempts to replace Colston's statue. Suggestions have included Paul Stephenson, a leader in the 1963 Bristol Bus Boycott; a mannequin of Jimmy Savile; Black Lives Matter protester Jen Reid with her fist raised; and even Darth Vader, as a nod to Bristol native David Prowse, who portrayed the fictional villain. For now, the plinth alternates between temporary art installations and periods of intentional emptiness, a blank slate inviting us to reconsider not just the statues, but the forces that elevate and dismantle them.

Personally, I like the empty plinth idea. Or perhaps they should put a mirror up there angled just right so that you see yourself projected up there on the thing and you can quietly ask yourself, *ought I* be torn down as well?

Swelling Discontent, Rising Confidence

The Global South, as historian and author Vijay Prashad and others define it, is not just a geographical marker, it's a political and economic designation encompassing nations and peoples in Africa, Latin America, Asia, and Oceania who have historically been on the receiving end of colonization, exploitation, and economic subjugation. This is not to say the nations of the

Global South form a unified bloc, but they share certain recent historical experiences that have shaped their position in the world system. And now, for perhaps the first time since the post-colonial independence movements of the mid-20th century, this collective is asserting itself in ways that are reshaping historical narratives and power dynamics.

During the 2023 United Nations General Assembly Namibia's ambassador, Neville Gertze, refused to let a German diplomat lecture his nation on reconciliation. "We will not be told about genocide by those who committed it," Gertze said, referring to Germany's colonial atrocities against the Herero and Nama people in the early 20th century. Namibia's refusal to accept platitudes from a former colonizer exemplifies a growing trend of former colonial subjects who are no longer content to play the role of silent recipients of moral instruction from the Global North. Instead, they're forcing the world to confront uncomfortable truths about the past and its lingering legacies.

Similarly, in Australia, Aboriginal elder Lidia Thorpe confronted King Charles III during his visit in 2023, shouting, "You are not my king!" Her defiant statement symbolized the ongoing struggle of Indigenous peoples against a colonial monarchy that continues to claim symbolic authority over lands it seized centuries ago.

At the time of writing, we are seeing more and more populations come to the defense of the Palestinian cause, in all of its forms of morally complicated resistance (don't worry, I'll get there). This particular conflict has become a symbolic vessel in which to pour long pent-up frustrations and an obvious flashpoint for the confrontation of the Global South and the power structures of neocolonialism and historical domination. This point of the symbolic nature of chanting, marching, or railing on about the plight of the Palestinians on college campuses and beyond is often misunderstood and unfairly cast as an antisemitic obsession with the behavior of Israel or

Jews. This charge, while blurred by the realities of historical antisemitism and European guilt, is becoming more cynical and obvious by the day.

Even more absurdly illuminating than these examples was the juxtaposition of then-presidential hopeful Kamala Harris proclaiming, "The United States of America is the role model of the world," just days before the largest BRICS summit in history convened in Johannesburg. The summit saw major expansions of the bloc, which now includes economic heavyweights like Saudi Arabia and key African nations, as it openly discussed plans to challenge US-led financial dominance with a new global reserve currency. For much of the world, Harris' declaration would have elicited little more than a bemused chuckle, a relic of an era when American exceptionalism carried unchallenged weight. In this new mood of global alignment and self-determination, such statements feel increasingly detached from reality.

The rise of the Global South, however, is only one side of the question as to why we are seeing revolt now. Those explanations will be the more intuitive explanations of the group. The Global South has plenty of obvious reasons to cause a stir. But if we flip the question over and look at the supposed wealthy Global North, the "internal" pushback against entrenched historical narratives is more striking, and for some, a bit more alarming and mysterious.

Chapter 5

The Anatomy of Upheaval

Why Now? Five Explanations

Explanation One: The Case for Progress

Let's start with an explanation that feels comforting and intuitive: progress. It's a favorite explanation for why this reckoning is happening now, and it goes something like this. As societies climb *something like* Abraham Maslow's hierarchy of needs, they begin to care less about survival and more about self-actualization, morality, and justice. Yes, I'm referring to that oft-Instagrammed index of human needs which Maslow himself never actually arranged into a pyramid. So, forgive me, Abraham, I'm merely borrowing the shameful misrepresentation for its intuitive appeal.

At the bottom of the pyramid are physiological needs: food, water, air, sleep. The absolute basics for staying alive. Next up is safety, security of the body, housing, stable income, freedom from physical threats. Once those second level needs are met, people start seeking belonging, relationships, community, family, love. Higher up, there's esteem, achievement, status, and the respect of others. And at the tippy-top, there's self-actualization, the kind of soul-searching work that leads people to meditate on their purpose in the universe or, say, challenge the ethics of putting slave traders on pedestals.

In the Global North, the case for progress feels plausible. Fewer people are living in survival mode compared to a century ago. Access to food, shelter, education, and healthcare has increased, allowing more time and energy to focus on higher-order concerns. Statues of men like Edward Colston stood unchallenged for decades, not because people didn't *care*, but because they had more immediate problems, problems that, to some extent, have been alleviated in wealthier nations. The story practically writes itself: material progress begets the opportunity to ethically question where all the material progress came from.

But the Case for Progress isn't limited to historical challenges in the Global North. It applies to the Global South as well, even in places where extreme poverty remains too widespread to comfortably apply Maslow's hierarchy in full. If the lower rungs of the pyramid, basic survival and safety, are still pressing concerns, then we might expect historical reckoning to be delayed. After all, if people are still fighting to meet fundamental needs, how can they afford the luxury of historical introspection?

Yet if we take the arguments of Steven Pinker and Hans Rosling at face value, progress is occurring in the Global South too. Extreme poverty is falling, literacy is rising, and healthcare access is expanding. But the reader should be cautious with these kinds of narratives. There is a way of absorbing them that quietly vindicates the current global order and the European-dominated arrangement of the world since the 1500s. This framing can end up excusing centuries of colonialism and its brutal legacy, not just on moral grounds but also by implying that, despite its horrors, it ultimately "worked." It suggests that pre-colonial societies were trapped in misery and violence until European systems – however clumsy or exploitative – came along and lifted them toward modernity. This is where Pinker's framing has faced serious challenges, especially on the topic of extreme poverty. Jason Hickel, for instance, argues that what we call "extreme poverty," defined as a lack of calories, shelter, and survivable material conditions, was virtually absent in many pre-colonial Indigenous societies. But if you begin your dataset after colonization and industrialization have already wrecked traditional structures and imposed new forms of scarcity, the narrative flips. It starts to look like Western civilization is solving the very crises it helped manufacture. Hickel's team used physical indicators like average height, health, and growth rates as more honest proxies for human well-being and caloric intake, measures that suggest a very different story than massively flawed GDP statistics alone that authors like Pinker lean on.

Still, I want to fairly present the Case for Progress as one explanation for today's upheaval. Despite the statistical framing and ideological sleight of hand, I think it is non-controversial to say that there has been real technological and material advancement in many parts of the world in recent centuries. And it's not unreasonable to say that, for millions of people, life has materially improved. Let's assume, at least for this argument, that overall material conditions are rising, and that some of this progress is genuinely reaching the ground.

So, if progress *has* indeed nudged millions of people in the Global South a step or two higher on the pyramid, the results aren't all gratitude for the Global Order and kumbaya for historical crimes. Instead, those small steps could be unleashing pent-up resentment. Decades or even centuries spent languishing at the base of the pyramid, too focused on survival to organize protests or political structures focused on historical injustices, may have created reservoirs of anger and frustration. And when those survival pressures ease even slightly, the door opens, not to a full "buy-in" for the system which has bumped you up from starvation and humiliation to "just enough" and scraps of dignity, but, instead, to the long-simmering demands for justice.

The unexpected outcome of the type of progress I'm alluding to in this explanation is that it doesn't necessarily lead to serenity and enlightenment. Instead, induced "progress," especially when perceived as unjust or undignified, can create fertile ground for revolt. The very metrics of progress that Pinker celebrates, declining poverty rates, increasing education levels, might coincide *directly* with uprisings against the injustices that those metrics cannot touch.

So, does the case for progress hold up? In some ways, yes. It explains why reckoning is more prevalent now than in eras when survival was all-consuming. But it also hints at a deeper tension: progress and justice and liberation are not the same thing. Progress can deliver material improvements while leaving systemic injustices intact and allowing those injustices to be protested more clearly, which ironically, might *be* an entirely different notion of "moral progress." As I'll explore throughout this book, the relationship between material progress and justice is anything but straightforward.

A final note, one that might help settle Maslow's restless grave after yet another misuse of his ideas on a pyramid. Maslow himself did *not* believe the needs he identified followed a strict, linear order. In fact, later in his life, he emphasized that his most elusive and slippery concept, *self-actualization,* which is often plopped atop the pyramid like a cherry, was *not* something that had to wait until you had a washing machine or a Starbucks on every corner. He saw it as something that was woven throughout *all* stages of life. This important clarification will reappear in all explanations. What Maslow was calling self-actualization, I may be calling the quest for moral integrity. And if that quest is thwarted or denied, expect a revolt at some point.

Explanation Two: The Case for Anger

What if the reckoning we're witnessing isn't about progress, but something more immediate and tangible: Anger. Anger at historical exploitation and the sheer audacity of a world that so often shrugs off its own brutal past. This isn't a new anger; it's centuries old, but now it's rising to the surface in ways that feel unavoidable, urgent, and deeply justified.

Pankaj Mishra, in *Age of Anger,* captures this fury, "It is impossible to ignore how the rhetoric of progress has masked the extraordinary violence of history." For much of the Global South, the promises of equity, freedom, and justice have been dangled like a carrot for decades, if not centuries, only to reveal a world order that perpetuates humiliation and inequality. Anger, Mishra argues, is the natural response to these broken promises, and it's a response that has been building for a very long time.

Consider the case of the Mau Mau rebellion in Kenya during the 1950s. For years, Britain's colonial government brutally suppressed the movement, detaining tens of thousands of Kenyans in concentration camps where torture and executions were routine. Though the British government formally apologized in 2013 and offered compensation to surviving victims, the acknowledgement came more than half a century late. The simmering anger over this period isn't just about the atrocities themselves, it's about the decades of stonewalling and the inadequacy of reparations that feel like an afterthought.

Or take the case of Belgium's recent return of a gold-capped tooth belonging to Patrice Lumumba, the Democratic Republic of Congo's first prime minister. Lumumba, a hero of Congo's independence and champion of a Pan-African vision, was assassinated in 1961 in a gruesome operation aided by Belgian and CIA complicity. And why, you might ask, did Belgium have his tooth in the first place? Because after Lumumba was murdered, his body was dismembered and dissolved in acid by Belgian officials, with one officer, Gerard Soete, keeping the tooth as a macabre souvenir.

Fast forward to June 2022, when Belgium ceremoniously returned the tooth to Lumumba's family in what was framed as a gesture of reconciliation. Jean-Jacques Lumumba, the hero's great-nephew, described the return as "a relief" and a moment that would allow the family and Congolese people to finally mourn. Yet, the act was met with widespread criticism in the Congo. Many saw it as an insultingly small gesture in the face of the systemic exploitation, atrocities, and theft Belgium carried out during its colonial rule. Headlines in Congolese media decried it as a hollow attempt at reparative justice. "Returning a tooth does not erase history," declared *Actualite.CD*. One Congolese journalist aptly noted that "symbolism is cheap."

So yeah, the case for anger seems somewhat strong here.

Even in the Global North, where many consider themselves distanced from the sins of colonialism or slavery, anger is bubbling over. Movements demanding reparations for slavery in the United States or the push to "decolonize education" in Europe reflect a refusal to accept the status quo. Apologies and gestures, when they come at all, often feel too little, too late, and the lack of meaningful action only adds fuel to the fire.

For instance, in late 2021, President Joe Biden signed a proclamation apologizing for the horrors of federally funded Indigenous boarding schools in the US, which systematically stripped Native children of their culture and inflicted widespread abuse. While the apology marked a historic acknowledgement, many Indigenous leaders responded by pointing out the absence of substantive reparative policies or federal commitments to address the lingering effects of this brutal legacy. For those living with generational trauma, a carefully worded proclamation is a small balm on a gaping wound.

When encountering the eye-popping forms of brutality inflicted upon the Global South in recent centuries, I find the *patience* and *forgiveness* to be quite remarkable. But it may be finally running out. And anger, an emotion which famously pairs with irrationality, demands action.

This explanation also deserves a nod to a demographic wrinkle; the waves of post industrialization immigration and shifting populations have brought descendants of historical crimes into the very geographies that once brutalized their grandparents. Many are now natural-born citizens, raised within the borders of former empires but carrying ethnic and cultural identities that are deeply entangled with the legacies of violence and exploitation. Some come from family trees with entire limbs that have been erased, shamed, or maimed. These histories aren't abstract or distant, but intimately woven into personal memory, family dynamics, and cultural dislocation.

A generation of so-called "third culture kids" now navigates this terrain, caught between the comforts of modernity and the unresolved wounds of history. It's no accident that many of the protesters who helped topple statues in Bristol were not white. And it's no mystery why certain conservatives seem so nervous about "importing anger" through their borders, even as their economies (pensions, currency solvency, and social security checks) depend on the labor and higher birth rates of the very immigrants they fear.

The larger questions, how to *address* historical injustice, what reckoning actually means, who owes what to whom, and what justice even looks like, will be taken up in the chapters ahead. But for now, let's let anger offer its clear, uncomplicated, and potent answer to the question, "Why now?"

Because people have plenty of reasons to be.

Explanation Three: The Case for "Woke" Confusion

Okay, I made it to the middle of Chapter 5 before dropping the "woke" word. I find the term exhausting. But there are valid criticisms embedded in what people mean when they invoke it.

Many of the thinkers I once found intellectually invigorating, some of whom I worked closely with on films or podcast series, bonded over a shared frustration with what became known as the "regressive left" in the post-9/11 era. And there *was* a real paralysis in public discourse when it came to criticizing certain cultural or religious practices.

Personally, I remember feeling uneasy when media voices repeated, "This has nothing to do with Islam," after the attacks. I understood the protective instinct behind the phrase. But it struck me as a sloppy noble lie, a kind of moral deflection that risked doing more harm than good. Of course, it had *something* to do with Islam, right? I mean, we could and should argue about exactly what that something *is* and *was*, and at what part of the so-called "radicalization" process it weaves itself into the justification, seeding, or motivation. But proclaiming the answer to be "nothing" felt like a tactical mistake. I mean, we could all see Osama Bin Laden reading directly from the Quran on our television screens, regardless of how slanted or strained his interpretations might be. Sure, it might shield some Muslims from prejudice in the short term, but it also might enrage the sort of bigot who senses dishonesty and lashes out harder at their innocent neighbors.

I fear that discrimination and danger to Muslims *did* happen over the next decades, and it continues to be a problem. And I do think the confusion of the "woke" contributed to it, if only marginally.

What I craved in the early 2000s was an honest conversation, one that could acknowledge the role a specific religion or ideology (any religion and any ideology) might play in shaping specific forms of violence without reducing whole populations to caricatures. I understood that to be a rather narrow needle to thread, but I thought it was important. But in academic and activist spaces, especially on my college campus, I often felt the presence of a moral forcefield, one that made it taboo to critique non-Western practices, no matter how ethically questionable. The understandable instinct was to push back against colonial superiority complexes. But shielding entire cultures and moral practices from scrutiny in the name of anti-colonialism can be just as distorting as the very ideologies it tries to resist.

So let me steelman this explanation: some of the upheaval we're witnessing today is, at least in part, driven by real moral confusion. But this confusion, especially among well-meaning, justice-oriented young people, deserves much more than idle mockery. It deserves to be understood. As you'll see throughout this book, I am very much aligned with those rowdy young people. The so-called "woke noise" is, to me, an earnest, if muddled, reckoning that would benefit greatly from a clearer understanding of its own philosophical foundations.

My interest in the post-9/11 conversation, including the film I directed, *Islam and the Future of Tolerance,* came from a desire to help sharpen that conversation on the left. The film, an adaptation of a dialogue between the prominent podcaster and author Sam Harris and the former Islamist radical turned reformer Maajid Nawaz, aimed to model how difficult conversations could happen across deep ideological divides. I was convinced by the urgency of warnings like, *"We liberals need to have this conversation honestly, or the right will have it for us."* Ironically, that warning came from Harris himself, who later failed his own test by embracing neo-conservative philosophy and promoting deeply misleading claims, particularly around Israel and its history.

So, are all those angry people tearing down statues and marching in the streets with signs that say "Gays for Gaza" just hopelessly confused about morality? Are they just romanticizing the Global South in a haze of guilt and historical revisionism?

The conservative historian Eric Kaufmann offers a tidy definition of wokeness as *"the sacralization of historically marginalized race, gender, and sexual identity groups."* But this definition misses the real moral problem. The issue isn't the sanctification of *identities,* it's the sacralization of cultural *practices* associated with those identities and the difficulty of separating those practices from the historical narratives of oppression wrapped around them.

In other words, we often feel like we can't critique a practice without indicting an entire culture, especially if that culture has been historically (or currently still is) brutalized. And that historical tension is the true heart of the confusion.

In the Global North, this battle has become especially intense. On the surface, debates revolve around facts: who did what, when, and to whom. But underneath, it's always a struggle over *moral* interpretation and moral narrative slotting. The questions are always about what those facts mean for how we think about justice, morality, and who gets to define progress.

Take the recent attempts to rehabilitate colonialism. Historians like Niall Ferguson and conservative pundits like Douglas Murray argue that the British Empire, while flawed, was a net benefit to the world, bringing law, infrastructure, and civilization. You should be hearing the deontology (woke sacralization of cultural practices) versus the consequentialism (net-positive outcomes) at play here.

The colonial nostalgia and moral shine was on display in a 2012 BBC docuseries called *Empire*, hosted by Jeremy Paxman, which culminated with this fascinating narration:

> *The sun had most definitely set on the empire. It had taken centuries to accumulate. It was gone in a couple of decades. The empire brought blood and tears and dispossession to millions of people. But it also brought roads and railways and education. There is no simple judgment to be made on three turbulent centuries of history. Once, the official line was that, apart from the odd blip, the empire was a good thing. Not just for Britain, but for the world. But the British grew ashamed of the empire and tried to wipe it from the national memory. The empire was certainly cruel, unjust, and unjustifiable if you were a slave on a plantation in the 18th century. But it was benign and humane if you were rescued from a slave ship by the Royal Navy in the 19th century. For good or ill, much of the world is as it is today because of the empire.*

You can hear the consequentialist logic humming beneath every word. Yes, there was suffering, but look at the infrastructure! And the final line as a hand wave taking responsibility for "much of the world as it is today" nearly pulls Steven Pinker and his flowery graphs about all the progress we've made into the screen.

But I can't help but point out a problem with just one of Paxman's talking points: education. At the time of British departure in 1947, India's literacy rate was a paltry 12%. Ghana in 1957? 5%. Kenya in 1963? 17%. Nigeria in 1960? 15%. Sudan in 1956? 16%. Jamaica in 1962? 39%. Today, nearly all of these countries have literacy rates above 75%, with many over 90%. It turns out the empire's civilizing mission wasn't all that committed to actually educating its subjects. But hey, congrats on all those railroads.

Still, I should remind myself that I am trying to grant the best-faith version of the case for moral confusion. And here is where I *do* think there is a valid point.

If the moral puritans and "woke mobs" (deontologists) light fire to the utilitarian logic of empire, call it all evil, and refuse to grant even incidental forms of technological progress, they risk falling into a moral binary. "If colonialism is entirely bad, then the colonized might be entirely good." And when the oppressed become sacred, their cultural practices often get swept into that sacredness. And in this process, we fail to apply universal moral standards to the victims *within* these cultures and tribes.

This is moral paralysis and this leads to real-world ethical blind spots. You can certainly bet that the Cognitive Dissonance Repairman is hard at work patching things up nicely here with tools about certain kinds of "ancestral" or "indigenous wisdom."

Let me offer a personal example. On a trip to Nepal, I visited a child goddess (Kumari) outside of Kathmandu. I had insisted on doing this when I "hired" a local guide to show me around for the day. He was reluctant at first, but after I endured an extended "sound bath" session at his friend's singing bowl shop, he may have felt like he owed me.

The experience was surreal. We waited outside a small room in a gorgeous wooden temple that was eerily devoid of tourists. I could hear someone, a young girl, playing alone on the other side of an thick wooden door. A guard tapped and whispered something through an opening. It must have been the signal that she was due to "perform" ... for me. Her playing ceased. I could hear some rustling of clothing and drawers sliding open and shut. And when the door opened, I was invited inside.

The room was a bare wooden space with a bed and a few chests, likely hiding whatever toys she had. She was dressed in a golden and red fabric gown and her very freshly painted makeup was flawless, tracing dark eyeliner to points near her temples which made them look much bigger and obscured her child sized eyes. She sat motionless on a wooden chair. My guide knew the rules. He removed his shoes, approached her reverently, and knelt at her feet. He prayed. Kissed them, bowed, and stood. She just sat. I didn't do any of that.

She was supposed to be the reincarnation of the goddess Taleju, chosen before menstruation and placed in this temple, her supposed spiritual home. I took a few photographs and smiled as non-awkwardly as I could muster. As the door closed behind us, and my guide straightened himself up, I lingered, listening, hoping to catch her transforming back into a child again on the other side of that closed door.

Of course, the whole tradition, belief, and ritual has a certain aesthetic beauty to it. And to my Western eyes and mind, an undeniable exotic "coolness" factor. But should we not morally critique the practice of child goddesses? Shouldn't we acknowledge that this tradition confines a child to a life (or at least a childhood) of isolation and objectification, completely at odds with her humanity?

But would I, a white Westerner, ever join a protest outside that temple? Probably not. That's the tension. It feels far more comfortable to protest an Israeli policy or a French immigration law than to critique something within the Global South. My last name buys me some leeway on the former. There's an implicit rule: don't punch down.

But this instinct, to protect the sacredness of the historically and globally oppressed, can lead us into real confusion and the mental trap of conflating critique of a practice with critique of a people.

Consider the tribal belief in some remote parts of Africa where I've filmed that children whose bottom teeth emerge first are cursed. Some of these children are abandoned or even killed. But critique this practice in the West, and you might be met with reminders of colonial missionaries pointing to "barbaric" practices to justify domination or "civilizing missions." The fear of sounding like them silences many today.

And that fear is not at all exaggerated. James Tobin, a notorious pro-slavery merchant, used these exact arguments. In his 1774 work, *Thoughts on the Abolition of the Slave Trade,* he described Africans as savages in need of salvation, "Their lives are a perpetual scene of bloodshed, superstition, and licentiousness." He cited their "heathen rituals" as justification for enslavement, bringing them to Christianity was framed as an act of mercy.

This rhetorical trap is still with us. If we criticize harmful practices today, do we risk sounding like Tobin? Is the only alternative to romanticize the very cultures that were brutalized? This is the confusion of the woke moment. But let's be clear, it's not just the liberals. The so-called "woke right" now mirrors the same dynamics, only flipped.

They scoff at identity politics while building their own around white Christian persecution. They mock safe spaces, but demand total protection from any critique of Israel while slinging slurs of anti-Semitism at anything that whispers the word "Palestine." They accuse progressives of over-empathizing with victims while insisting *their* national myths remain sacred.

By now, the reader should be attuned to this pattern. It's the moral hypocrisy game all over again. Consequentialist when it suits them, deontological when they need purity principles.

And both "sides" are now fluent in the swap. When a term like "woke" reaches this state of moral seesaw madness it quickly loses its luster, functional meaning, and purpose. And I suspect my readers are just as bored with the label as I am writing about it.

To move forward, we have to get better at disentangling cultural behaviors from historical oppression in our moral positions. We can acknowledge legacies of trauma without letting them blind us to present-day harms. This isn't easy. But it's the only way to build an honest moral vocabulary that transcends political posturing and performative outrage.

The crucial point, and where I return to my defense of the rowdy "woke mobs," is the distinction between a moral position, a political one, and an underlying theory of human nature. We'll have more time to unpack those categories in the chapters ahead. But for now, it's important to recognize that holding a negative moral judgment about something like the child goddess tradition in Nepal *does not imply* support for bombing or sanctioning or even making a public declaration about the moral position.

Beneath many of the flimsy debates around "wokeness" lies a deeper, often unspoken, theory of what it means to be human, a distinctly leftist (as opposed to liberal) proposition that places justice and dignity at the heart of any conversation about progress. Simply put, a leftist theory of human nature assumes that a sense of justice, and an honest and genuine cultural reckoning with the wounds of injustice, is a *necessary precondition* for any kind of durable, meaningful progress.

If that theory is correct, then yes, real moral progress would require grappling with historical and moral injury *before* attempting to "fix" individual practices like the child goddess ritual. That's a far more coherent defense of the "woke left," and I'll return to this argument in full later in the book. But if I can help it, I won't use the word "woke" again.

So, my verdict: does moral confusion explain part of this reckoning? Yes. But it's not a left-wing phenomenon. It's a universal habit. It's a broken compass we've all tried to use. And it's not going to help us find true north unless we stop switching our moral frameworks every time the political winds shift.

Explanation Four: The Case for a Moral Awakening

Let's start by acknowledging why this explanation is so attractive. It flatters us. The idea is simple and seductive: that we are just better people now. More moral. More awake. That's why we're protesting injustice and tearing down statues. That's why we see so clearly what those before us were blind to. Compared to those who celebrated Empire Day in 1905 or shopped for cotton spun by enslaved hands in the early 1800s, we believe ourselves to be morally evolved. But this explanation, however appealing, is built on a shaky foundation.

The comforting story that humanity just changed their mind about the horrors of slavery and injustice, that we all stretched, yawned, and saw the light (please appreciate the lengths I'm stretching to distinguish this usage of "woke"), is both historically misleading and morally unhelpful. It allows us to judge the past with smug detachment, as if our moral superiority were inevitable. Were the ancient Greeks, the American plantation owners, or the British slave traders of the 17th century really in some kind of ethical coma?

The utilitarian moral philosopher Peter Singer gives us an image of expanding moral concern that is helpful here. In his famous model, our ethical circles begin with our kin and can expand outward: from family to tribe to nation to stranger to all conscious animals and ultimately to entire ecosystem. There's some truth in that story of a process of expanding moral concern over time, although it is a story which is constantly abused by those who are interested in pushing a jingoistic form of Western or Judeo-Christian bias where "unenlightened" tribes were overly distrustful of extending moral consideration to strangers.

But let's grant truth to the model and recognize that, over time, it seems we have widened the circle of who deserves our empathy. But what actually drives that expansion? Is it simply moral enlightenment? A sudden awakening of conscience? I doubt it. A better answer lies in the constraints and permissions and awarenesses created by technology, and in what tools we have available to manage our cognitive dissonance.

The moral arguments against slavery, exploitation, or injustice have been publicly made for centuries. But I would argue they are embedded in us existentially. I am positing that, of course, deep down, we've *always known* slavery is a moral abomination. So, why did it take so long to formally toss it into the "moral waste bin of history"?

This is where our Cognitive Dissonance Repairman reenters the picture. One of the most potent tools he uses, across eras, is the appeal to necessity. "We had no choice." "This is how the world works." "The benefits are just too great." These narratives dull the sting of moral discomfort. And so, entire ideologies about race, natural order, or divine mandate are erected as fortresses to shield us from the true dissonance. Now, imagine what happens when the Repairman starts losing his tools.

Consider the invention of the cotton gin, not because it ended slavery immediately (it definitely didn't, in fact, I'll explain why it got much worse and more brutal before it ended), but because, over time, mechanized cotton processing began to chip away at the justification of necessity. The most compelling Repairman's line "we have no choice" sounded weaker. In the moral subconscious, slavery no longer was a regrettable but essential evil. It just looked like evil. That's not moral awakening. That's a shift in the available justifications. That's a technological event exposing a moral lie you can no longer believe.

Let's make the example even more primitive: say you're a very early human who needs to haul heavy rocks from a riverbank to your cave every day. It sucks. Your back hurts. It's tedious. Then you spot another guy, he looks a little different, maybe talks differently, and you decide it's more convenient to make him carry the rocks for you. So, you force him. And with your extra leisure time you start to think of some improvements for the world. Over time, you start believing he was meant to do it. Maybe he's inferior. Maybe your god told you this was the natural order. Maybe his ancestors did something wrong and now he owes you. These are all repair jobs to soothe the tension between your convenience and your conscience.

Now enter someone else with a simple invention: a wheelbarrow. Suddenly, you no longer *need* the guy. You can do the labor. It is trivially easy. The justification that "there was no alternative" collapses. But the system doesn't vanish overnight. There's inertia, culture, economics, and religion. You've built statues. Your priests have created rituals. Your neighbors have done the same. Maybe you're afraid the guy will take revenge if you free him. Maybe you've spent decades convincing yourself that what you're doing is not only normal, but good. Giving that up might even spark a war. That should all sound familiar.

But still, in moral terms, the invention of the wheelbarrow removes your best excuse. And let's say you actually then free the strange looking slave and start encouraging your angry friends to do the same. From the outside, it might look like you had a moral epiphany. But inside the system, what's really changed is the landscape of justification. The wheelbarrow has stolen the Repairman's toolkit.

Let's bring this back to Festinger's experiment to clarify the point. My contention is that when it comes to something as extreme as enslaving another human being, almost no one is *consciously* operating in the $20 group. Remember, Festinger showed that if you pay someone a large enough reward to lie, they can justify the lie to themselves as being "worth" it while being fully aware that they are lying. But that experiment involved a trivial moral infraction. Slavery isn't trivial. It would take far more than twenty bucks — a million? A trillion? — to *consciously* justify it as a necessary evil which was "worth" it. And even then, I'd argue the math equation *still* collapses. With something this severe, almost everyone functions like the $1 group. That is, they *don't experience it as a moral infraction at all*. They convince themselves it isn't wrong in the first place. There is no dissonance to repair because, in their minds, there's nothing to fix.

I want to make sure that point lands because it is quite scary and deep. Sometimes, the greater the infraction, the more horrible it is, the more morally repulsive and wrong, the more likely it is that people will be in the $1 dollar group (*successfully* lying to themselves about the moral rightness of the thing) than the $20 dollar group (consciously lying and having awareness about the immorality). This $1 dollar group is in for a much more difficult self-reckoning, *if* they ever get there.

Now to be clear, this isn't the whole story. I do believe genuine moral awakenings *can* happen, even without new technologies. Sometimes, ethics precede technological invention. Sometimes a moral stance and argument becomes so powerful that we invent new tools to align with it and enable more of us to shift to the $20 dollar group and then easily escape it when the technology crashes that simple economic equation. I'll explore the two paths of escape from Festinger's experiment in the following sections.

But we need to throw some cold water on the notion that deep, species-wide moral awakenings just bubble up spontaneously, like enlightenment falling from the sky. That's just theology in disguise. It's Moses and the stone tablets all over again. And frankly, I don't think anyone needed a carved rock to figure out that killing was probably bad. Monty Python, eat your heart out.

So, am I really saying that most people, across time, would have rather *not* practiced slavery if given the choices that *I* have at my disposal? Yes! I think the average human has an aversion to cruelty. But, scarily, the structures of justification — economic, religious, social — are powerful enough to override that discomfort. We create gods, laws, politics, historical narratives, and identity myths to protect ourselves from the agony of knowing we are doing harm. And those stories are often extremely good at doing their job of protecting us from moral shame.

I'll return to this fascinating relationship between technological progress and moral reckoning, but for now, notice that we live in a time of unprecedented visceral *exposure* to injustice and cruelty (regardless of their frequency). Colston didn't see images of chained bodies. Empire Day wasn't interrupted by live footage of amputated limbs. But we *do* see these things. Our phones vibrate with horror. Our feeds bring us closer to the consequences of cruelty. And that triggers our cognitive dissonance constantly.

Would slavery have lasted as long if the people of Bristol in the 1700s had been bombarded with videos of its realities, even as they enjoyed their cheap tobacco and cotton? I don't think it would have. But again, that's not a moral awakening. That's a breakdown of denial, and we should be prepared for violent explosions of cruelty and doubling down in the last stages when the horror is so plainly revealed to us that we have been in the $1 dollar group of cheap moral sell-outs all along.

Analysts often cite the Vietnam War as a turning point in public reckoning, when the horrors of conflict began reaching the public in near-real time. Iconic images like the "Napalm Girl" were developed, printed, and circulated within days, landing in newspapers, magazines, and living rooms across the country. These images were morally emotionally disruptive. They placed average Americans into their own version of Festinger's lab and our mental assembly line photo handling by the journalist, historian, and philosopher was working overtime. They were forced to reckon with a brutal contradiction between their moral instincts and the justifications they'd accepted about domino theories, freedom, or anti-communism. For some, it no longer held up.

But today, we are drowning in Napalm Girls. Every day, our phones serve up hundreds of images and videos from Gaza, Sudan, Ukraine, and elsewhere — raw footage, often more immediate and intimate than anything printed in *Life* magazine. And yet, for many, the moral rupture *doesn't* come. The contradictions don't provoke widespread dissonance, or if they do, the response isn't collapse, but entrenchment.

Why?

Here, the final stages of Festinger's $1 group become especially illuminating. When people are deeply committed, when their justification is internalized and moral certainty is woven into identity and wrapped in ideological narrative, the arrival of more horror doesn't break the spell. It tightens it. The worse the atrocity, the more fiercely one must cling to the idea that it isn't actually wrong, or that it is somehow justified. The images don't force reevaluation. They trigger defense. And the viewer doesn't wake up. They double down. And as terrifying as this is, they also might go on a rampage to "kill the witnesses" to the truth of their moral failings. This can take the form of murder, or suicide, or both. I mean those things literally of course, but also figuratively with a kind of moral suicide which is permanent retreat into ideology or willful ignorance, and a kind of moral murder as shunning and casting out family or friends who are too much a reminder of the deeply buried moral truths.

Explanation Four Continued: Crashing Out of the Experiment

Neoliberalism and its utilitarian logic have conditioned many of us to live in the $20 group, training us to see every moral dilemma as just another trade-off. We don't deny that there are real moral problems and violations that happen out there. But it tells us as long as the benefits outweigh the costs, just cash the check and carry on. But this only works until the equation starts to break down which can happen in one of two ways.

Sometimes the *reward* loses its value, like with the invention of the wheelbarrow, or the cotton gin. At that point there is no way to lure you into a bad moral deal because the offer is just not very enticing, or rare, or technologically impressive anymore. Are cotton T-shirts all that great?

And sometimes the moral *cost* becomes too glaring, like a body in the rubble, like the Napalm Girl, like Hind Rajab, like images of emaciated and starving children, or disabled teenagers burnt alive in their wheelchairs. In this way, even if you are told the benefits are huge, you just can't swallow the cost.

When the $20 logic stops holding for either reason, cognitive dissonance comes roaring back. And at that point, many people don't leap forward into moral clarity and exit the lab. They collapse backward, into the $1 group. They convince themselves there was never a problem at all. That the horror is justified. That it's actually moral, or even divine. This is the birthplace of ideology, theology, supremacy identity, and nationalism.

Notice exactly where in that psychological process narrative justifications tend to appear, whether they're religious, genetic, or historical. They often don't lead, they follow. Slave owners, traders, and even everyday consumers of slave-produced goods were surrounded by cultural, economic, and religious narratives that dehumanized Africans. These functioned as large-scale Cognitive Dissonance Repair mechanisms, helping entire populations maintain the patently absurd but necessary fiction that Africans weren't fully human. That fiction allowed the "I'm a good person" gear to keep turning.

Individuals may be born into environments where these stories are already deeply embedded in sermons, history textbooks, and community rituals. On an individual level, someone might absorb racist or hierarchical thinking long before ever meeting someone enslaved who clearly laughs, cries, loves, and wonders, just like any other human, strangely enough. So, yes, within that individual process, the narratives and justifications and beliefs precede any direct cruelty. But what I'm talking about here is the broader sociological arc. From that vantage, these justifications emerge to stabilize and soften the psychological tension created by more basic and potentially shameful forces, desires for cheap labor, power, unreasonable security, or control. The stories ride in *after* the fact as post-hoc rationalizations, making the entire arrangement more palatable.

I hope this section is read with precision, especially by my intellectual foes (many of whom were once friends) who insist that the deepest and most troubling initial source of human conflict is ideological. I'm thinking of Sam Harris who stands out as a relentless proponent of this view. For decades, he has argued that religious beliefs and civilizational values are what truly drive human behavior. The basic takeaway of his theory is that "belief governs behavior." I've mentioned that I directed a film which featured Sam, and I later wrote and produced a ten-part archival series that traced a decade of his conversations and debates across topics ranging from neuroscience and free will to moral responsibility and Islam. I know his arguments well. And I don't disagree with the premise that beliefs govern behavior. Of course they do.

But what I'm pressing on here, and what's too often left out of that analysis, is the functional role those beliefs play. They aren't just worldviews passed down or thought up. They're patches. Tools. And they are often wielded in service of holding together a moral self-image when actions start to contradict it. Even the racist who grows up swearing by genetic hierarchies, or the religious nationalist who preaches divine order, may belong squarely in the $1 group. They're covering the gap between what they are doing and what they need to believe about themselves in order to live with it.

I'm not saying we shouldn't take people's professed beliefs seriously. We should. And I'm not dismissing the sincerity of their beliefs either. They are absolutely consciously sincere. But we should also interrogate what those beliefs are doing and notice how they're serving to reduce dissonance.

How seriously do we take the belief of the student who claims to have discovered a deep love for peg-turning after pocketing the dollar and lying about it? I suppose, for reasons of kindness or compassion, we might want to be charitable and delicate when doubting how "real" that student's new belief is, but we have good reason to doubt the weight of it or the mysterious reason why it formed. Belief governs behavior, yes, but that doesn't mean belief is the *starting* point. And if it isn't the starting point, then persuasion alone may not be the antidote to dangerous beliefs. You don't fight peg-turning ideology by proving that peg-turning is boring. You do it by naming the incentive, tracing the dissonance, and refusing to fully buy into the performance of sincerity.

For a more disturbing example, consider Muhammad Atta, the lead hijacker of the 9/11 attacks. He clearly was espousing a religious ideology aligned with Bin Laden's interpretation of the Quran by the time he flew a plane into a building. But we can not overlook the fact that he decided to seek out Al Qaeda the day after Israel bombed and killed 107 Palestinian civilians who were sheltering in a clearly marked UN tent in Lebanon.

And to be abundantly clear, I am not *dismissing* the *danger* which certain very angry people pose who might be enraptured by certain beliefs. I am not proposing a full denial that people really believe in heaven or hell or paradise or genetic supremacy or that God gave them specific tracts of land. But I think, if my analysis is right, the anger will be understood more clearly, and the danger will subside.

The ironic danger here is that someone like Harris is engaged in the very same psychological patch work which I am talking about here. The utilitarian ethics which dehumanizes and objectifies with phrases like "collateral damage" serves as a tremendously powerful way to smooth over the moral nightmares inevitably produced by his ideological stance. I'll return to the idea of ideology in Chapter 9 and present it as the true enemy of moral integrity.

And, though it's difficult, we should also notice the faint good news buried in all of this ugliness, that people often *need* to successfully lie to themselves in order to do harm ($1 group) is still better than a world where harm is done consciously, casually, and without resistance ($20 dollar group), or worse, the psychopaths, who might do it just for fun. Luckily, they are rare.

So what I'm urging us to do, what I believe is possible, is to crash through that final defense. Don't stop at the $1 group. It's the most dangerous place to get stuck. Let the dissonance stand. Don't repair it. Let it break you open, and build something better on the other side.

But crashing through isn't some grand moral awakening, though it might feel like that. It's recognizing what you *already knew deep down*. You had a feeling this thing was wrong, out there, in the background, under the surface. And now, for whatever reason, the conditions have shifted just enough to let you admit it. The illusion breaks. The dissonance is exposed.

And the reward for finally seeing it clearly? Well ... drumroll, please. In film or literature, this moment is known as a title drop.

Explanation Five: The Case for the Insufficient Reward

Here is my most revolutionary suggestion so far: that a primary reason we're living through a moment of upheaval is because more and more people are starting to realize they've been cast into the role of Festinger's $1 group. And they don't like it one bit. There's something quietly devastating and encouraging about this realization.

I've already hinted at the basic framing of the problem, the trade-off model we've been living in. I'll restate that plainly. But I will also widen the lens and pull history back into the analysis to show how this logic applies not just to our personal discomforts, but to the deeper existential layers beneath them.

First, the familiar part.

Imagine standing in one of those over-lit, overly symmetrical lifestyle stores. Everything white, glowing, minimalist, and strangely dead inside. On display is the iPhone 18. Its impossibly smooth edges, the triple-lens camera, the AI-driven promises of clarity and speed. You pick it up, turn it in your hand, and feel that little thrill, that engineered flicker of anticipation. But then, without warning, your mind flickers.

Cobalt.

You didn't ask for that thought, but there it is, like a push notification from your conscience. You remember something. A headline you saw somewhere. A photo that one of your annoying leftist friends shared on their wall. A story about the Congo. Kids mining with their bare hands, their lungs filled with toxic dust, their lives funneled into the global supply chain so that this miracle of engineering can sit in your palm.

You try to shake it off (or your Repairman does). You didn't build the system. You didn't write the rules. You're just a person in a store buying a phone like everybody else. You shrug, pay, and walk out. But the feeling has changed. The excitement's thinner now, like biting into food that smells delicious but tastes like ash. And that question, subtle, unwelcome, starts to creep in again: *Is this enough?*

That question doesn't end with the phone. It spreads. It stretches across the whole rhythm of modern life. The workdays filled with meetings and inboxes. The nights spent scrolling. The weekend trip booked with points. The new kitchen gadget, the craft cocktail bar, the dopamine jolt of a sale ending in three hours. It's a system that mostly works, if you play it right. You feed it your time, your energy, your attention. And in return, it spits out little prizes. New devices. Nice dinners. Curated experiences. Achievements. It's not misery. It's not failure. But even when the rewards show up on time, something in them feels thin.

It's not just that the game is hard to win. Sometimes it's not. Sometimes you win. You get the thing, the upgrade, the carefully assembled life. But more and more people, even when they're winning, are feeling a strange undertow. A sense that the prize doesn't land. That the pleasure is somehow diluted. That the reward, while technically delivered, isn't quite doing the job. Not because it's too small, but because it carries with it the quiet weight of the bargain that made it possible. And the more clearly we see the trade-offs — moral, environmental, human — the harder it becomes to pretend that the deal was ever clean.

In a way, this part is just simple economics. Perhaps the rewards just need to be better to calm these questions? Perhaps the instability of the future needs to be better dealt with by the social contract of governments and economic systems? Perhaps the answers here are just political and economic in nature. Vote blue. Vote red. Vote tie-dye. All true enough. But that's not really the point I'm trying to put forward.

Utilitarian morality begins to break under too much clarity. It's easy to accept a distant cost for a local gain, but not when the cost is staring back at you through the screen, or in the dust-filled lungs of a child halfway around the world. The trade-off falters. And when it falters, the reward is hollowed out from the inside.

And this sentiment is no longer niche. It's spreading, surfacing in jokes, in memes, in that viral image of a parent telling a child to "go play outside" while the "outside" they've built is a stretch of strip malls, beige sidewalks, and parking lots. Even the best-case version of the world is starting to feel ... off.

But this is just the surface.

Because as destabilizing as it is to realize that today's rewards feel empty, there's a deeper shift underfoot, one that turns not just on what we're being offered now, but on *how we got here at all*. The more explosive version of the Case for the Insufficient Reward isn't just about the "progress" of the present. It's about the legacy it's built on. The past doesn't vanish. It hardens into wealth, property, structure, and systems, and that means every single so-called reward today is tangled in a web of *historical* trade-offs and unpaid moral debts.

Don't despair. All is not lost once we make these claims. But first let's understand them. This is where the idea of ***unjust riches*** comes in. And to really get it, I want to walk you through a little parable.

Imagine you're a taxi driver. You take your car in for a routine oil change. At the same time, another customer brings in a car just like yours, but they've prepaid for a massive overhaul: brakes, engine, transmission, the works. You leave the shop, and while you are gone somehow, the mechanic mixes up the vehicles and starts doing all the expensive work on your car instead.

You get a call. The mechanic says, "Just giving you an update. Everything's covered, we're about halfway done." And right away, you realize there's been a mistake. But you don't say anything. You nod, you approve the work, and you walk away thinking you just got a major upgrade for free.

You go pick up your car and it runs smoother than ever. The other unlucky shlub arrives at the shop and realizes the mistake and is pretty miffed but the mechanic can't do anything about it. Let's say it was the last day the shop existed for whatever reason.

So, this guy takes you to court to fix this mess. And the court hears the case and you're held accountable on account of the concept of "unjust riches." The court finds a compromise, maybe you pay back half the cost, or something like that. You didn't cause the mistake, but you knowingly benefited from it, and the legal system finds some way to level the scales. It's not perfect, but it feels like justice was generally served. We feel a kind of moral equilibrium is met in the end and everyone can walk away from the mistake feeling decent enough. Justice.

But now imagine another scenario where there is no court. There are no avenues of appeal. Perhaps there are racist or classist barriers to these institutions. Perhaps they are just corrupt. Doesn't matter. The point is the other guy is stuck with the broken car and out of cash and he can't afford to pay again. He misses work. His income dries up. Maybe he loses his job altogether. His family struggles. All the while you and your taxi business are thriving and raking in money and prestige. The effects ripple out from this one unresolved injustice. One man's quiet benefit becomes another's ongoing collapse.

Now, let's take it even further.

Years pass. You keep working, keep growing your business. Your family does well. Theirs doesn't. Then one day, decades later, one of their descendants stumbles across the old mechanic's records. They put it all together, the mix-up, the injustice. The way their family's decline began with a simple, overlooked mistake, and moral infraction.

But now what? What could be done? Could *you* go back and fix it? Could you calculate the rides you gave with that unjustly repaired car? Could you trace all the money you made, the houses you bought, the college tuition you paid, all from the compound interest of that one moment of silence?

Probably not. It's too late. The damage is already buried in layers of time and consequence. And yet, for the descendant who discovers this, that doesn't make the resentment disappear. In fact, the *impossibility* of resolution might make it worse.

Now imagine the logic of this toy universe is zoomed out across continents and centuries. The "taxi repair coverup" becomes land stolen, labor exploited, bodies trafficked, histories erased, genocides. The families that benefited don't always know how. They just know they're doing well. The families that suffered might not even know exactly where it began, but they feel the weight. And justice, which might have once seemed possible, now feels out of reach.

So what are we left with? A world where one group rides in a smooth car that shouldn't have been theirs to begin with and another walks. That's what is meant by unjust riches.

The key insight here is to notice that justice has a window of opportunity. It opens, and it closes. And once it closes, it becomes very hard, sometimes impossible, to reopen. You might already be thinking of things like reparations for slavery, or the right of return for displaced people. These are classic examples. When the window is open, there's at least the possibility of repair. But when it's slammed shut, the original harm doesn't vanish. It doesn't fade with time. In fact, the resentment often festers. The residue of injustice deepens. And sometimes a rock comes flying through that window.

This is what makes the awareness of unjust riches so volatile. The world is thick with them. And many people, many systems, seem to know this on some level. You can see the strategies unfold: stall the conversation, change the facts on the ground, wait out the clock. If enough time passes, perhaps the memory itself will become too distant to act on and the gravity of time will gently close the window as generations multiply. But others are keeping track. Others are watching the windows of justice close, and they are not forgetting. And they are with ever more frequency discovering old closed windows in histories which are often intentionally buried and obscured. That tension and discovery is fueling much of the upheaval we're living through now.

The ways these frustrations surface aren't always graceful. Sometimes it's an indigenous land acknowledgement read at the opening of a conference. These are delivered like rituals that know their own powerlessness. Sometimes it's more awkward: a viral video of white teenagers kneeling to kiss the feet of Black classmates in an attempt to confess generational guilt and make an apology for a slave owning distant ancestor. These moments are easy to mock. But I think they deserve more than that. They're clumsy, yes, and sometimes "cringe" but they're signs of a larger moral anxiety: the realization that we are living amid unresolved, compounding injustices, and no one knows quite what to do with that knowledge.

That's what I see, too, in signs like "Gays for Gaza." Not mere confusion, but connection and solidarity. A persecuted group (or a group which is having success in its quest for justice) extending its moral imagination to another group whose window of justice is still cracked open, just barely. These moments can be misunderstood and they often are by unserious conservative commentators and agitators. They can look like incoherence if you're unwilling to consider that justice isn't bound to identity or territory. If you miss that, you're likely to laugh, scoff, or write it off as the same old moral confusion. But I don't think that's what it is.

I'm not offering this concept of unjust riches as a doomsday revelation. I know how overwhelming it sounds. It's tempting to shut it down as impractical or paralyzing, like I'm proposing a universal, unfixable guilt or unshakeable sin. But I'm not.

Yes, I believe unjust riches are real, inescapable, and foundational to much of the modern world. I believe they're a major reason why the rewards of our current system often feel spiritually bankrupt, even when they look materially rich. But that doesn't necessarily mean we're doomed. This is just the condition of a strange animal which can propose counterfactual moral universes in the past, present, and future. And I think we're capable of facing it.

The Case for the Insufficient Reward is not a theory of collapse. It's a theory of refusal. A refusal that begins not in politics or economics, but in the honoring of one's moral integrity. A refusal to be satisfied by a world that makes us flee from our best moral selves for the sake of toys we don't need, jobs we don't love, and futures we don't believe in.

And this aspect of the upheaval is, I believe, the most hopeful thing I've ever seen.

Chapter 6

Tomorrow's Morality, Today!

The allure and danger of appealing to historical moral vindication

Everyone's Favorite Judge

"History will be the judge."

Whether it's whispered by revolutionaries, echoed through the halls of political power, or casually and confidently presented in online debates, it carries an almost mythical weight, the sense that the speaker has somehow borrowed the gravitas of time itself to strengthen their point. And why wouldn't they? History, after all, doesn't interrupt. It doesn't argue back. And it somehow always agrees with you. It's the perfect audience, infinitely patient and unfailingly silent, until, presumably, the day it isn't. Until the day it casts its unflinching, definitive verdict whether we are around to see it or not.

Nelson Mandela, in his post-apartheid South Africa, told his audience, "History will judge us on the extent to which we have used the freedom we won." George W. Bush, during his farewell address amid the turbulence of the late 2000s, confidently reassured Americans that "history will judge the decisions made during these times." Stalin, never one for understatement, declared in a 1941 radio address, "History will not forgive us if we do not now do our utmost to save mankind." Martin Luther King Jr., with characteristic hopefulness, offered the moral arc of history as a comfort, "The arc of the moral universe is long, but it bends towards justice." Malcolm X, in contrast, spoke with fiery conviction. "History will see that we were right." Mao Zedong, on the cusp of founding the People's Republic of China, proclaimed, "History will judge the significance of our revolution."

Online commentators on opposite sides of the Palestinian cause, Ben Shapiro (again, seriously, no relation) and Owen Jones, both frequently invoke it. Ben has an entire book entitled *The Right Side of History*. Owen has frequently rattled off the phrase "History will not look kindly upon the perpetrators of this crime" while referring to an overhead photograph of an undignified and dehumanized process of aid delivery after an Israeli blockade.

Barack Obama evoked the idea of history as a stern reminder while reflecting on climate change when he said, "I refuse to condemn our children to a planet that's beyond fixing. I refuse to be part of a generation that leaves a stain on history."

And then there's Adolph Hitler, of course. In 1939, addressing the Reichstag, he confidently asserted, "History will judge who was in the right."

So, will it?

What the Future Knows and What the Future Has

When we appeal to history, we're not really making a statement about the past or the future. We're making a statement about ourselves, about our desperate need to believe that our actions are part of something larger, something meaningful. And perhaps more importantly, we're hedging our bets. It's a kind of moral insurance policy, a way of soothing the ever-present fear that we might be just as flawed, just as fallible, as those we now judge.

We tend to confuse and entwine moral progress with technological progress because they both feel like they move us "forward." Technological progress, unlike moral progress, is something we *can* objectively quantify, define, and measure. It's essentially the ability to manipulate the physical world in order to align with our intentions. That might sound fancy, but it's just a way of saying, if I want to shuck all these ears of corn, I need a method for doing so. I can do it by hand — manual labor *is* a kind of technology — but I can also build a machine that runs on fuel and does it faster. That machine is just concentrated, targeted energy shaped and harnessed to match my intention. If technological progress is about harnessing energy to *actualize* our intentions, then moral progress is about *understanding, examining, and better aligning* those intentions to our best possible selves.

Technological progress is relatively easy to track across time. We write it down. We document it. It spreads. It rarely disappears. If I whisked you off in the time machine and dropped you into a random city with no other information, you could probably guess what century you were in just by observing the tools, materials, and systems around you. I'm sure that brilliant ideas have been forgotten, erased, or lost. But in general, technological progress behaves like something you can graph. It has a shape.

Now, compare this to the way we sometimes talk about moral horror. When people encounter injustice, cruelty, or absurdity today, they often say things like, "I can't believe this is *still* happening" or "Are we really *still* doing *this*?" or the more sarcastic, "What year is it?" These reactions are telling. They reveal the assumption that moral awareness ought to advance on the same timeline as technological capability. That we should "know better by now."

And when someone says, "One day, everyone will admit this is wrong," they're drawing on the same intuition. What they really mean, especially when we bring in the theory of cognitive dissonance, is something like: "Eventually, a kind of moral technology will be developed that renders the Repairman in all our heads obsolete – and we'll all be forced to admit what we've secretly known all along. That this is *wrong*."

But now I want to flip the usage of these phrases.

Because the reverse instinct also exists. Sometimes people fully *agree* that a moral horror is happening. They aren't denying it. But they believe that in the long run, history will vindicate the choices being made. That the suffering now will produce a better world later. That future generations will look back and thank us for making the hard decisions. In this version of the expression, we are pulling the lever on the trolley so that others may live well down the tracks. We bear the stain now, so they can live clean.

And once again, history becomes the ultimate consequentialist validator.

Moral Atrophy and the Dark Gods of Consequentialism

Consequentialism has a strong appeal. It tells us that morality is a matter of outcomes, that the ends justify the means, and that if the scale of good is large enough, the moral price is worth it. But this imagines history as a kind of invisible calculator which tallies costs and benefits, and ultimately rewards those who contributed to the sum total of progress.

This is a comforting idea. But also a dangerous one. Because once we imagine history as the final judge, we begin to justify all kinds of present-day harm in the name of future good. We start outsourcing our moral reckoning to a fictional arbiter. We tell ourselves that future generations will thank us, even if we have to break a few things now. And in doing so, we turn history into a kind of **dark god**. One that accepts sacrifice today in exchange for promised absolution tomorrow.

This dark god, we Americans tell ourselves, has already blessed the psychologically tellingly named "Greatest Generation" for saving the world during World War II. They dropped one atomic bomb, then another, and told themselves it was necessary. I'm not claiming to know whether that was ultimately true, but I do know this. Whatever came after, no matter how stable or prosperous, should not be used to justify what happened. It's a mistake to think the present can morally absolve the past.

To lean on history as a moral authority is to risk substituting self-serving myths for genuine moral growth. This reliance on historical justification fosters a kind of **moral atrophy**. Instead of confronting dissonance directly and strengthening our integrity, we defer to self-justifying outcomes. Instead of asking,

"Is this right?" we ask, "Will it work?" And if the answer feels good enough, we let ourselves off the hook.

Of course, this critique isn't a rejection of consequentialism outright. In Chapter 9, I will contend with the objection that I'm sure many readers are thinking about the *reality* of "having no choice." And in those moments, if they *are* real, you may be forced to drop bombs I suppose. My grandfather was on a ship headed toward Japan when he heard the news that Truman had dropped the bomb. He told me more than once that Truman "saved his life." He said if he ever passed Truman's grave, he'd bend down and kiss it.

It's a common refrain to point to historical moments of massive moral compromise like this and justify them by saying something like, "If they hadn't done that, we'd all be speaking German or Japanese now!" Of course this is not just a nationalistic expression but also a reference to the "values" that those two languages at that moment represented, and how they may have delivered me a crummier life. This history-leaning consequentialism plays a powerful role in our moral lives.

But I was born in Pennsylvania. And I speak English, not German or Japanese. So, all good, right? Well, I'm quite sure there may have been people not too long ago who would've had a very similar kind of conversation – if only *they* had had an atomic bomb or two.

Prophets, Poets, and Presidents: The Two-State Solution

~~~

The heat clings to the lawns outside Grouseland, Governor William Henry Harrison's mansion in the Indiana Territory. It's July 12, 1810. We are in a humid clearing under a canopy of sugar maples and hickory trees. The sweet smell of tobacco smoke and fermenting hard cider barrels is already in the air.
~~~

African slaves move with purposeful efficiency, preparing for the assembly. One kneels at the garden's edge, pulling weeds that threaten to strangle the neat rows of flowers. Another sweeps the gravel path leading to the porch. Nearby, a boy polishes Harrison's boots. Slavery here is technically illegal under the Northwest Ordinance, but Harrison has long advocated for its legalization. These contradictions aren't lost on anyone watching, least of all the slaves themselves, who overhear murmurs about today's meeting with Tecumseh and his warriors.

You've been sent here as a government scribe, tasked with documenting the proceedings. Though not a newspaperman, you've often wondered if your notes might one day find their way into public discourse. It's been dawning on you, and perhaps others, that events like these are threads in a larger tapestry, a story that's starting to take shape which will one day have a name: Manifest Destiny. The term hasn't yet gained currency. It will be another 35 years until a journalist named John L. O'Sullivan will coin the term in *The United States Magazine and Democratic Review*.

The sentiment of this unnamed ideology is unmistakable though, even in 1810. It's currently dressed in the language of treaties and negotiations. What you record, at a single flash point negotiation, of that larger wave which you can sense may one day serve as a reference for some author of moral philosophy trying to piece together this movement's origins.

The grounds are bustling. Settlers, officials, and soldiers mingle, their conversations hushed but charged. Soldiers, muskets in hand, their presence a not-so-subtle reminder of the imbalance of power, their eyes frequently darting toward the tree line.

Then, a shift in the air. A faint sound — the rhythmic rustle of leaves, the crunch of feet against soil. It grows louder, steady and deliberate, until the figures emerge from the edge of the forest. Tecumseh and his warriors step into view, their arrival freezing the assembly. They move in measured formation.

You had never seen Tecumseh before, though you had heard plenty. Whispers of his name carried stories of cunning and ferocity, of brutal uncivilized, un-Christian, tactics in battle. Scalped soldiers, villages reduced to ash — these tales painted a portrait of a savage warrior, a man born from the chaos of the wilderness. You told yourself these stories were exaggerated, propaganda designed to stoke fear. Yet as you see him now, tall and broad-shouldered, his piercing gaze sweeping the assembly, you can't deny the aura of dangerous intrigue that surrounds him and his deerskin coat, the eagle feather in his hair, his very posture. For a moment, the quiet hum of the cicadas fades, and even the rustling of the tall summer grass seems to still.

Tecumseh glances toward the mansion, his eyes landing briefly on a young African boy standing at the edge. The boy's small hands worked quickly as the sun climbed higher in the sky. Now, he watches Tecumseh and his warriors with a mix of curiosity and caution, his dark eyes wide, his body still. Tecumseh's expression hardens, a flash of disapproval, though it's not directed at the boy. His critiques of slavery are well-documented, denouncing the practice as a moral stain and a violation of natural law. His condemnation of the white settlers' contradictions is not just philosophical, it is deeply personal, aimed at the hypocrisy of a society that speaks of liberty while perpetuating bondage.

This world in Indiana, with its rigid hierarchies and harsh conditions, is likely the only one the African boy has ever known. Perhaps he wonders what it would be like to walk freely among these warriors, to be unshackled from the constraints of servitude. Or perhaps the thought doesn't occur to him at all, his reality too deeply entrenched to imagine an alternative.

You are not blind to the arguments that justify this system. They are as common in the taverns and churches of the territory as the air itself. Slavery, the argument goes, provides order and discipline to those incapable of managing their own lives. It is said to bring civilization to those who would otherwise live in chaos. You have heard settlers defend it as a necessary evil, and some even claim it as a positive good. You're not sure what you believe about these things. You're here to document, not to judge — or so you tell yourself. But watching a glance between the African boy and an Indian warrior, you feel a knot in your stomach. Is it guilt? Is it shame? Or simply the weight of witnessing something that will be debated for generations to come?

Tecumseh stands tall, his voice deep and deliberate as he speaks (not in English) to a translator who had been plucked from the fur trading ranks. Tecumseh's words carry the weight of generations, denouncing the treaties Harrison claims are legitimate and proposing a clear solution. Tecumseh wants a boundary that would preserve the lands of the tribes around the Great Lakes for the Native nations, free from further encroachment. This idea, a kind of proto-nation, had been debated in taverns and among settlers for months. Some dismissed it as absurd; others saw it as a dangerous challenge to American expansion, and few trusted that the natives would stay confined to their proposed borders, claiming that this would simply create a savage, hostile, and barbaric state adjacent to theirs. Still, others whispered about a more radical solution: a single state, for white settlers alone, with no place for the tribes who had lived there for millennia.

"This land is not ours to give away," the translator relays, Tecumseh's voice rising with intensity. "It belongs to all of us — our children, their children, and the Great Spirit who entrusted it to us. If we allow you to take one piece, you will take another, and another, until there is nothing left. The sales you claim to have made with tribes were illegitimate and forced through bribery and the haze of alcohol." His words are met with murmurs from the settlers. Some shift uncomfortably; others fold their arms and glare. Harrison's expression remains neutral, but his hands are clasped tightly behind his back, his knuckles white.

You continue to write, documenting the increasingly obvious breakdown of these "negotiations." There was little illusion that a real ceasefire was going to be reached today, but the foregone conclusion of an escalation of violence still fills you with fear now that it is solidifying in ink.

You look at the African boy, to Tecumseh's hardening face, to Harrison's righteous pose, you wonder how "history" will judge these days. Will it record Tecumseh as a freedom fighter or a hindrance to progress? Will it see this particular meeting as a chance for peace squandered, or simply as another step in the relentless march westward where the natives failed to accept the generous diplomacy of the settlers? Would there be a native nation around the Great Lakes on future maps for school children to debate with their own flag and mythology? Would the technological progress of the world of 2025 look a certain way so as to clear up all the moral ambiguity you were feeling.

As you glance around the assembly, your eyes are drawn to a particular man standing just behind Tecumseh. There's something about him — an intensity that feels different, darker. His eyes burn with a quiet, simmering rage, his jaw set as if biting back words he longs to shout. You pause for a moment, lifting the pen to re-dip it, before leaning toward a fellow observer to whisper a question. They tell you his name: *Tenskwatawa*. Tecumseh's brother, the man they call "the Prophet." You've heard stories about him. He claims to have visions of divine favor. He gives fiery sermons condemning the settlers as the spawn of scum. They say he preaches that the Great Spirit has charged him to restore the land and rid it of corruption.

Watching him now, you can feel the sting of his anger, a force that seems to emanate from his rigid frame. In his mind, you sense notions brewing of gods and divine orders of violence, a theology forged in desperation and hope. His presence is a contrast to the measured rhetoric of Tecumseh, and you wonder if these brothers represent two sides of the same coin: hope and fury, diplomacy and violent resistance. If peace is to be achieved, it must reckon with both their visions.

As the meeting progresses, the tension is palpable. You wonder if the settlers, who hold the upper hand in both arms and political leverage, even see this as a negotiation or merely a formality before the inevitable encroachment. Yet you write it all down, knowing that these moments may someday become the foundation for others' understanding of what happened here.

You realize that the responsibility of documentation is as much about asking questions as recording answers. What defines justice? Compromise? Coexistence? What would peace even look like in a place where every tree and river feels claimed by two opposing truths? You sense that these questions will not be answered here today, but perhaps they will echo into the future, waiting for someone – another voice, another vision – to try again.

Speaking English and Historical Morality

William Henry Harrison would become president. Tecumseh would die resisting him. His brother, Tenskwatawa, would turn toward prophecy, fire, and holy vengeance. The movement would unravel. The land would be taken. The Native American struggle for survival would be reduced to footnotes, to mascots, to silence.

And then I would be born, on nearby land, 172 years later. I would speak English, rather than the Shawnee that Tecumseh spoke, or Umani that the Lenape people spoke who inhabited the land where I was born. My life would be relatively safe, I would attend good schools, and grow up believing that slavery had long been abolished and history had already been judged.

Is that a problem? Was the language I spoke a big deal?

It's not a simple question. But it's a necessary one. Because it gets to the rotten root of consequentialism. If the end justifies the means, then almost anything becomes justifiable.

Let's be extreme. Imagine the Nazis had succeeded. Imagine they had conquered the entire planet, eliminated every non-Aryan, and created a unified global German speaking Reich. You might say, "But then *I* wouldn't exist," and that's true, but that's just a silly statement. None of us know exactly why we exist. The real question is, what if you *had* been born into that world, I suppose as an Aryan baby? You might look back in horror when conducting historical research (if you were allowed) and discovering how your world came to be. You might feel the weight of that inherited brutality pressing down on your conscience. But I just did that about the world I was born into. And I can recognize the brutal erasure of Native nations that cleared the way for ... me?

But saying "it could have been worse" is not a moral position. It's a cope. It's 17th-century philosopher Gottfried Wilhelm Leibniz's infamously appalling argument, that this must be the best of all possible worlds, because a loving God wouldn't allow otherwise and this blend of evil and good must be balanced just right for his divine purpose. Frankly, I think we can do better than that God. And Voltaire agreed by savagely mocking it in *Candide*, where the character Pangloss parodies Leibniz's position by insisting, even amid horrible disasters and human suffering, that "all is for the best in the best of all possible worlds."

It's not hard to imagine a counterfactual present where Native American resistance succeeded, and Manifest Destiny never took hold. Maybe, in some alternate timeline, a time traveler shows up with crates of advanced weaponry and smallpox vaccines. Maybe the outcome flips.

And given which of the two "civilizations" were practicing more egalitarian politics at the time, I have to wonder, if you were *forced* to choose "moral" sides, honestly, which would you have rather defended?

The borders on today's political maps would look different. And no, I can't guarantee they'd be more prosperous according to Steven Pinker's bar graphs. But that's exactly the problem — progress graphs are a terrible lens for historically evaluating moral decisions. Japan is a technological marvel today. Is it "better off" because Truman dropped two bombs? That's not a moral question. That's just statistics posing as ethics.

My grandfather told that Hiroshima story often. My mother grew up hearing it more than the rest of us, I'm sure. Interestingly, she visited Japan for the first time only recently. At the Hiroshima Peace Memorial, she had to walk out, emotions overwhelming her. Perhaps, in that moment, the great historical cognitive dissonance repair job — the one that tries to patch over atrocity with graphs and flags and English speaking — finally started to fall apart.

I've spent most of this book showing why consequentialism and deontology both fail. Why neither tells us what to do when we're alone with a decision that history won't be around to grade. Why they keep us trapped in a hypocritical seesaw — one side claiming moral duty and principle, the other claiming moral payoff, both somehow complicit in the same injustices.

But I haven't yet told you, plainly, what I think we need *instead*.

That changes now.

Chapter 7

Timeless Integrity and What Evil Feels Like

Why everyone has faced the same fundamental moral dilemma … and always will

Love Not Logic

I saw her online profile first. She was stunningly beautiful. There was no ignoring or avoiding that. It was on a site that allowed for fairly extensive writing and profile building rather than the quick swipe. I liked what she had to say, of course. There were all the right markers of good taste in indie music, a counterculture and intentional orientation toward life and exploration. A word jumped out in the *about me* section, "conviction."

Then my eyes went over to her basic back-of-the-baseball-card stats: age, height, religious or nonreligious label, and then, there it was, "vegan." I was not one of those. I'm sure my profile listed me as an omnivore. I had always generally agreed with the vegan arguments in principle. I grew up with dogs, I had them as pets, I loved animals ... and I also ate them. To be honest, I didn't think much of it when I sent her a rather lame message (she still gives me grief about this today). I was fairly certain her profile was dormant, and I didn't want to waste time crafting anything too elaborate.

But she replied. And suddenly, my elaboration improved significantly. She seemed lovely, and a date was set.

This is not a romance novel, so I'll spare you the cheesy details about falling in love or the voices in our heads telling us we'd be together. The point is, I was very into her. On that first date, when veganism came up she was slightly sheepish about her reasons for it. I didn't really understand why at the time, but now I know better. Putting forward a reasoning based on an ethical commitment and animal suffering rather than, say, health or environmental motivations, tends to turn people off. They (and their Repairmen) really hate feeling judged or made to feel bad. But I told her that moral conviction was the best reason and that I had always agreed with the ethical arguments. I meant that. But I had never really tried it. This is probably the moment she fell for me. I told her I'd try to do it. I'm not sure if she believed me or not. But she also probably had no idea how in love I was with her already.

And I never consumed animal products again.

Well, that's not entirely true. A few days after that first date I ordered a slice of buffalo chicken pizza without thinking. It was an automatic habit at one of my favorite foods at a sloppy New York City pizza shop around the corner that I'd probably ordered from dozens of times. I think I was three bites in before I realized what I was doing. I took one more bite, then threw it away.

That bite of pizza was seven years ago. And that woman is now my wife, and this book is dedicated to her. I've been an enthusiastic (and much healthier) vegan ever since. I've fallen in love with not just her, but with food and flavor itself, as well as cooking.

So, what happened to me here?

In my intellectual and philosophical capacity to analyze the situation, this was a move in a moral direction. I am convinced that eating animals, even if they're raised, killed, and processed in more "humane" ways than the industrial horror show of factory farming, is an immoral and unnecessary action given my circumstances. According to the Sentience Institute, approximately 99% of farmed animals in the United States and 74% globally are raised in factory farming conditions. When including farmed fish, the global figure rises to around 94%.

But here's the thing. I always *knew* that. I always agreed with it. So why didn't I align my behavior with my thinking? Convenience? Cowardice? Addiction? Conformity? Cost? Biased health arguments? Naturalistic fallacies? Probably some combination of all of them.

And why did I eventually align my behavior? Well, if I hadn't met this incredible woman, someone I admired and wanted to impress, I don't know if I ever would have changed. And that's why I consider my personal shift in dietary practices to be a missed opportunity to cultivate my moral integrity even if it was a move towards morality.

The process *could have been* an honest confrontation with cognitive dissonance. Thinking about factory farming, learning more, paying attention to my internal deliberations and machinations, entering a conversation with my Repairman. And finally adjusting my behavior. Instead, it was a different story. Love motivated me. Perhaps that's the only variable I needed to succeed.

The important thing to notice in this story is that a utilitarian (one who factors in nonhuman animal suffering) would argue that there's no problem with this. *Anything* to get fewer animals killed, right? That was the *consequence* of the story. Let's make veganism fashionable, trendy, or dare I say, romantic. There is a rather racy and controversial ad from PETA which shows a split screen of two couples having sex where the "meat eater" finishes too quickly and results in a disappointed and sexually frustrated woman kicking the man out of her apartment while the "vegan" half of the screen shows a very not-at-all-disappointed woman enjoying a longer sexual experience. The tagline at the end of the 30 second ad is "Last longer. Go vegan." (By the way, there *is* some correlative evidence for this claim based on improved blood flow and lower cholesterol.) But the point is the utilitarian vegan advocate would be thrilled if this ad "worked" in the way of hijacking people's strong motivation levers, like the sexual lust of young men in this case, to result in saving as many animals as possible.

But this chapter isn't really about animal ethics. It's about moral integrity.

Perhaps you're vegan, or perhaps you're not. If not, I'd encourage you to pay close attention to the emotions you might have felt while reading this section. Maybe the Repairman in your head is at work, defending your diet. Eating habits happen to be one of the most emotionally and morally charged subjects. But I hope you don't get stuck in that. I'm telling this story not to preach to you or argue with you about eating animals, but to humbly admit a missed opportunity.

Better Worlds and Feeling Nothing

Since making this shift, I've engaged deeply with animal ethics. I've watched horrifying videos from slaughterhouses, visited sanctuaries, and interviewed activists. My wife's veganism began, she told me, when a friend showed her videos and she read more about what happens behind the closed doors of slaughterhouses. The cognitive dissonance sparked by those difficult videos was enough to push her out of Festinger's Lab within a year or so. I think she has quite a rare psychology.

Philosophers such as Peter Singer and Martha Nussbaum have suggested that future societies may look back on our treatment of animals with the same moral disgust we reserve for historical atrocities like slavery or genocide. Nussbaum, in her work on animal rights and capabilities, argues that ethical consideration should extend to all sentient beings, emphasizing the moral failure of ignoring animal suffering, while Singer's work in Animal Liberation critiques speciesism, the prioritization of human needs over animal suffering, as an ethical failing. My engagement with the arguments have solidified my view that the animal food industry represents a moral nightmare — a systematic, normalized cruelty on a massive scale.

But again, the point of this chapter is not to convince you to be a vegan. You can disagree with these arguments. You can resist them and shield yourself from them with successful deflections and counterarguments, I'm sure. That's fine. The point of me presenting them is to tell you that I, *personally*, agree with them, and when I look back at my own participation in what I contend is a horror show — nearly every day for decades — I realize something chilling: *it felt like absolutely nothing to participate in it.*

This mundane indifference is precisely what Hannah Arendt described with her famous concept of the "banality of evil." The automated, mechanical, dissonantly-repaired, and unexamined nature of our minds enables cruelty to persist without *any* inflated emotions like anger, shame, or malice. I wasn't angry. I wasn't malicious. I wasn't tortured or in any semblance of intellectual discomfort. I was simply hungry. And then, I ate things that tasted great. But if I *had* taken a careful moment to look, or think, I contend that I would have naturally been struck by some level of discomfort.

And that's why I call this a missed opportunity. It wasn't a lack of knowledge. Of course, I knew where a piece of calamari, or cheeseburger, or slice of bacon came from. I'm sure you do too.

So, the world got "morally better" from the vegan utilitarian lens. PETA estimates that I saved 200 animals a year by falling in love with a vegan and following in her footsteps. That's a great moral result, no matter the reason it happened. But did *I* get "morally better"? Did I get the "right" to draft this chapter and deliver statistics about animal suffering in a section which some of you must think is sounding smug already? Did I become a "better person" by doing something "better" for animals or the environment or whatever?

Those are the questions I want to focus on. And those are the ones I want to universalize beyond the surprisingly emotionally fraught issue of eating animals.

What We Say, What We Do, What We Feel

A 2023 Harris Poll, shared by *Fast Company*, revealed that 77% of Americans aged 35 to 54 — primarily Gen Xers and older Millennials — expressed a desire to "return to a time before the Internet and smartphones dominated daily life." Even among younger adults aged 18 to 34, 63% shared this sentiment. Overall, 67% of respondents across all age groups wished for a less digitally connected era. You have probably heard friends or family, or yourself, say the same thing. "Life was better back then," they say, "before the endless scrolling, before our attention was torn into a thousand fragments."

Yet those same people will sit down to dinner with their phones on the table and will scroll through apps while they tell you how much they hate doing it. And of course, I use my phone far "too much" too. I do not wish to preach to you from a plinth of purity here.

This is the paradox of revealed versus stated intentions. Our *revealed* intentions are what show up in our behavior, the number of hours we spend online, the choices we make when no one is watching. Our *stated* intentions are what we claim to want: to be more present, to have deeper conversations, to live more meaningful lives. In the modern world of data and capital, revealed intentions are given far more weight. They are measurable. They are monetizable. They can be turned into charts and profits.

But can throwing out *everything* other than the revealed intention really capture the truth about human motivation and the human condition? Are we simply to look at what we *do* and declare that this is who we "really" are, and that all else is just virtue signaling psychobabble? Should we just simply observe our own behavior in order to learn who we really want to be?

In his 2017 book *Everybody Lies*, Seth Stephens-Davidowitz called Google search data a kind of "digital truth serum." He showed how unfiltered search queries revealed the things people truly fear, crave, or wonder about, often far more honestly than they would admit in surveys or even to their therapists. From about 2000 to 2015, a period where few people worried that anyone was monitoring their Internet usage, this window of "search bar candor" may have captured an unusually raw portrait of the modern psyche. Stephens-Davidowitz had access to all kinds of Google, Facebook, Shopping, Dating, and

Pornography search data. This can paint a rather dark, if not honest, picture of the human mind as well.

And we have built an entire economy on this paradox of revealed and stated intentions. The tech industry thrives on exploiting this gap.

In 2006, Facebook replaced its simple "Wall" with the "News Feed." The Wall had been a basic, chronological list of posts from friends. The News Feed introduced an algorithm that ranked posts based on engagement, showing users not just the latest updates, but the ones most likely to keep them scrolling. It also surfaced posts from friends of friends and incorporated ads and promoted content designed to maximize clicks.

The public hated it. Or at least they *said* they did. Thousands of users and students protested, calling it invasive and manipulative. They accused Facebook of spying on their activity and reshaping their online experience. But the observable data told a different story. Engagement soared. Users clicked more, scrolled more, and became more deeply trapped in the new feed.

Mark Zuckerberg had seen this pattern before, of course. In 2003, while at Harvard, he had launched Facemash, a site where students were shown two randomly selected classmates and asked to rate who was more attractive. The site drew immediate outrage over privacy violations and objectification, but that did not stop students from using it obsessively. Actions once again betrayed words.

So, what should we conclude? Do we truly want endless dopamine loops and bottomless feeds? Or are we simply failing to resist systems that are designed to be irresistible and are not overly concerned with some silly philosophical conversation about "moral integrity" and becoming our "best self"?

The tension between what we do and what we wish we would do is not a new problem. Søren Kierkegaard described it in his 1849 work *The Sickness Unto Death* as the "despair of possibility," the agony of being overwhelmed by the gap between who we are and who we imagine ourselves becoming. He wrote, "An individual in despair wills desperately to be himself. But being oneself is exactly what he cannot do." This is a timeless human struggle. But modern technology makes the despair more acute.

The recent pandemic lockdowns revealed this for many in the West too. How many of us used to say, "If I only had the time, I'd write that Great American Novel ... learn to play the cello ... pick up that old acrylic paint set again." And then, we were granted the gift of time, and the cello sat in the corner, mocking us. How many of us defaulted to doom scrolling, streaming, and distraction? Of course, a potentially deadly pandemic and massive economic uncertainty throws a rather influential variable into this experiment about revealed intentions. And, I know for many, the experience of COVID was not always a walk in the park, but I would venture that for a decent number of my younger and relatively healthy readers, it was (literally).

But does this mean that a dusty cello means we really never wanted to chase those philharmonic dreams? Or is there much more psychological complexity at play here, fear of failure, fear of disillusionment, or simple defeat to immediate micro-gratitude of the like button.

I am reminded here of a passage Kurt Vonnegut once wrote in his pseudo-biographical masterpiece *Timequake,* about a parakeet named Wild Bill. Wild Bill would spend hours squawking and rattling the bars of his bird cage, trying in vain to escape, and annoying the daylights out of his owner, Kilgore Trout. One day, Trout sets the thing by an open window and unlocks it. But Wild Bill remained on his perch, suddenly falling silent. Trout nods and slowly closes the cage again and says, "Good! Now you've still got something to hope for," as Wild Bill goes back to yelling at the bars.

We might not be so different.

The fight to encounter our deep fear of the braided relationship between freedom, morality, and responsibility, which I've emphasized in all of the chapters of this book, is the thing which characterizes the human condition. This is the eternal struggle between comfort and conscience. The fight will persist forever. But I worry that the fight, in modern times, is not very fair and that is what is being deeply reflected in the polling data I began this subsection with.

We know we carry a kind of dual nature. On one side, we are shaped by the biological imperatives of evolution, tuned for survival and reproduction. But survival is not the same thing as philosophical flourishing. In fact, the drive for survival can, beyond a certain point, morph from a prerequisite into an enemy of our deeper capacity for reflective moral life.

Evolution instructs us to shift behavior when we sense threats. When predators are near, or when we perceive that they are, we react accordingly. We narrow our focus, prioritize safety and survival, and become more competitive or defensive. But in the modern world, many of the systems we inhabit function as artificial predators. They are designed to *ensnare, capture, and consume* our attention and exploit our instincts, keeping us reactive rather than reflective.

But this inner self which strives for philosophical flourishing is difficult to measure and observe from the outside of any system. To an outside economist or political scientist tracking human behavior, the data simply records what people do. It is then assumed to reflect what people genuinely want or believe, and disregard the occasional counter-desire poll.

I worry that much of our modern socio-political structure, and, in particular, the leading role we have given to free-market economists and technocrats since World War II, is generating a world that we cannot resist, not one that we truly want.

This is why I do not accept the simple framing that revealed behavior shows us who we "really" are. Of course behavior matters and sometimes observing our own behavior does reflect some kind of inner truth that we have been shielding ourselves from. But sometimes, oftentimes, the *exact opposite* is true. Revealed behavior does not mean that our highest, most courageous selves are not real, or that our moral potential is a lie because we often fail to enact it.

We all carry what philosopher Harry Frankfurt in his 1971 essay *Freedom of the Will and the Concept of a Person* called "second-order desires." We *want to want* better things. We *want to want* to write the novel. We *want to want* to resist the scroll. We *want to want* to be kinder, braver, more present.

Say we redeploy the image of your mind as a system of gears, all turning and generating whatever physical behavior is happening. There is the gear of self-image, reflecting who we *appear* to be in our behavior. And there is the gear of *aspirational image*, that fragile best-self we dream of becoming. We all wish we could get the teeth of that gear to interlock so that our aspirations would turn the machinery of our lives more often.

But the Repairman inside us does not want this. This aspirational gear is something extra and nonessential to the functioning of the system. The Repairman is a lazy bastard. If he has already patched things up well enough that you feel fine and the gears are generally humming along, he's content to sit back and relax. If you are not in pain, if you are not in crisis, the Repairman is perfectly happy to lounge around eating bacon sandwiches all day while your aspirational gear rusts on the axle.

Yet around that lazy Repairman, there is the pulse of integrity. A philosophical hunger to live in such a way that what we say, what we do, and what we feel are no longer so painfully out of step.

Of course, I know I am painting this entire picture a little too simply and righteously. If it were that easy, I would have gone vegan years before I ever saw the smile and beautiful face of my future wife on a dating site.

The fight to align our better selves with our behavior is not fair, and it is not easy. It never has been. Long before the billion-dollar attention economy was built to knock us into a comfortable stupor of "good enough," this was already a tough fight. But even if you set all of that aside, there are other forces at work. There are all the ways we tend to convince ourselves that striving toward our better selves is foolish, too difficult, impractical, and naive. And far too often, we forfeit the bout before it even begins, as we retreat away from the effort to cultivate moral integrity back into the defined, measured, and predictable world of first-order survival desires.

The Mundane Dilemma

In Chapter 3, I briefly previewed what I called the "mundane dilemma." It's mundane not because it lacks importance, but because it's so oppressively commonplace in our modern economic system.

Let me illustrate this with a personal story. In my early post-college years, I was struggling to find steady work and paying inflated New York City rents. I took freelance video editing jobs wherever I could find them for clients ranging from makeup brands to college bookstores looking for a video component to their super exciting annual industry meeting. All the while, I had some awareness of proving to myself and my often-nervous father that I could "support myself" with a degree in Film Studies rather than pursuing something more stable and predictable, like the information technology and pharmaceutical career path my older brother had chosen.

Like many young people, I was armed with half-baked critiques of the seemingly inhumane socioeconomic system I was about to enter. Some of these ideas were rather uncontroversial. I thought that the big cigarette companies were pretty bad. That shouldn't come as a huge shock. It was the year 2000, and the exposés of their behavior were well-documented. But those companies also had a lot of money. Money I could definitely use.

So, what would I have done if one day I received an email from a major agency, offering me six figures to direct an ad campaign for a cigarette brand? A few months of work for a life-changing amount of money. Would I have said no?

Let's fly into my mind at that hypothetical moment. You can hear the gears crunching. The whole system might even lock up. But here comes the Repairman, armed with his tried and true consequentialist tools, "The money is good, you have no choice but to pay your rent." "You can donate some of it to a good cause!" "Your father will finally respect your life choices." "Hey, maybe you can even sneak in some subversive messaging into the graphic design." "Listen, lots of great directors do this kind of thing. Even Errol Morris does Chipotle commercials!"

These are the same tools that were at work when we considered the Black actor faced with the offer to play the stereotyped role on a hit show. For anyone over 18, the dynamics of this dilemma, if not the amount of money, should be so common to be, well, mundane. Some might read this and think, "if only I were to get so lucky."

I never faced this specific mental crunch. I never got that email from Philip Morris. And sitting here now 25 years later, I can *say* that I would have turned it down and smugly scoff at those who don't. But can I really be sure? I mean, I definitely wasn't vegan back then.

We All Start at Zero

There is no way to predict the details of the moral decisions you will face during your life. Some will be big. Societal, civilizational, historical. Others will be small and immediate, what you eat for dinner tonight, whether you should toss that guy a nickel in the subway, whether you should accept that job offer from the oil company. But the point I want to insist on is that the nature of the dilemma is always the same. Each one is a chance to encounter your cognitive dissonance, ask difficult questions, and ultimately self-evaluate.

In Chapter 9, I will deal with the most common way we try to escape this responsibility — the classic "I had no choice" response. But here, I want to emphasize something simpler. Only you can handle the honest evaluation of these questions.

Perhaps you really *love* the taste of animals. I do too. So, I *think* I get it. But I'm not you. I cannot climb inside your experience and weigh exactly how much ecstatic pleasure you feel when you eat them. That experience carries its own kind of moral weight, which only you can judge. Maybe, in your mind, that pleasure is worth a million dollars on Festinger's pegboard. Or maybe it is worth one dollar which might be true if there is no perceived moral violation at all, since your Repairman is doing a great job convincing you it is fine. Again, that is the trickiest part of the entire moral psychology conundrum. And again, no judgment from me if that is what you are feeling. I did the same exact thing for decades. But actually, I take that back. I have *some* judgment, including at my former self. Or at least a level of disappointment.

Because the only defense we have against this kind of rationalization is to cultivate our moral integrity and the balance between honesty, discipline, and self-forgiveness. And with practice, it can grow stronger. The muscle can "unatrophy." And because every moral encounter works the same way, this strength can carry over to other parts of your life.

I have spent much of this book examining huge historical moral questions: slavery, colonization, child labor, silence in the face of genocide. These may feel "easy" to oppose in the abstract. But in real life, they do not present themselves cleanly as simple moral propositions. They arrive tangled in relationships, in culture, in pressure, in self-interest. And it can be much harder than we realize to see them clearly, let alone act with courage.

For example, you never faced the exact moment of being handed a birthday gift, a hand-knit beautiful sweater from your sweet-faced grandmother, who smiles and tells you it was knit from cotton. And you know that cotton was picked by slaves. I never faced that moment either. But plenty of young men and women did face exactly that in the 1800s. I would like to say I would have refused it, explained my moral objection, and invited her to march with me in a dangerous and unpopular abolitionist rally the next day. I *want* to say that.

But that young man accepting the sweater with a smile also never faced the exact crisis of wanting to play a stupid game on his phone while working on a chapter about moral philosophy. Of course, he had his own analog version of this dilemma. Maybe a candlelit quill-and-ink poetry session was fighting for his attention against a particularly heated game of hoop ball, or whatever passed for irresistible distraction in the mid-1800s. But that is exactly the point. The *analogy* of the dilemma is the same.

Because I *did* face plenty of moments where my grandmother handed me a roast brisket at a holiday dinner, which she had slaved over in the kitchen all day, and I gladly accepted it. I ate it without hesitation. And it felt like nothing.

And recently I attended my nephew's Bar Mitzvah service which concluded with the entire congregation, which was made up of my family friends, being asked to stand and turn towards the Israeli flag and pray. I had to quickly wrestle with the cognitive dissonance of that situation which could have gone in several directions, not wanting to embarrass anyone, not wanting to stand out "like a jerk," wanting to display my objection as an example to the younger boys and girls in the congregation. In the end, I quietly excused myself from the service and waited in the lobby. But if someone had stayed in the room and simply stood and remained quiet, or even uttered the words of the prayer, I can't really fly into their mind and morally evaluate the bravery or cowardice of their internal deliberation. All I know is what I was able to do in that moment. And all I can do is encourage others to attempt to be honest and attentive to their own struggle, rather than to ignore, downplay, or erase it.

But it is important to note that these small entangled mundane psychological moments are exactly the material that things like genocides, slavery, and animal farming are made of. The big clear clean historical moral dilemmas which end up "telling the story" were always made up of little humans wrestling with little moments and smiling grandmothers holding sweaters.

And again, I hope it is clear that I am not drawing a moral equivalence between something like human slavery and animal farming or accepting a job with a cigarette company. That is not my point here. The point is this, the *structure* of the moral encounter is the same. In all cases, the knowledge of the moral violation is there, and the argument for the necessity of the practice does not hold enough water to float. The opportunity to face a difficult choice and navigate it with honesty and courage, or to slide past it, is what repeats. That is the pattern, no matter how large or small the moral stakes may be.

And *if* there is a moral score to keep, it is not based on which particular dilemmas you are lucky or unlucky enough to face. It is based on how much growth you can experience in the face of the ones that *do* appear. You do not get to choose the puzzles. You only choose how you solve them with the knowledge you have at the time and an honest evaluation of what you can emotionally handle, which is usually *much* more than your Repairman wants you to believe about yourself. That is what matters.

Some of us are born into constant moral challenge. Some are born into limited moral opportunities. But we are all born with the chance to discover the limits of our moral integrity. And in that sense, we all start at zero.

And on the topic of keeping score, we need to clear up another utilitarian habit of moral self-evaluation.

Why the Karma Bank Is Empty: The Fallacy of Moral Ledgers

The idea that morality operates like a ledger — a cosmic account where good deeds can balance out bad ones — is deeply ingrained in how many of us think about ethical behavior. This metaphor assumes that acts of kindness or charity can somehow compensate for acts of harm or selfishness, as though morality were reducible to a fungible unit. It's a comforting idea, but it is fundamentally flawed. Morality, in the way in which I would like for you to think of it, does not work that way, nor should it be cumulatively evaluated that way.

Each honest encounter with our cognitive dissonance and the ensuing moral wrestling match is a passing clash which presents itself a fleeting opportunity to engage, retreat, shrink, ponder, shrug, or grow. It is not transactional. The growth of integrity cannot be measured as a series of pluses and minuses on a moral spreadsheet.

The idea of fungibility is useful here. A "dollar" is fungible. Any five dollars from your wallet can repay a five-dollar debt, no matter which bills you use. Energy, too, is fungible. Solar energy can pass through a leaf, a cow, a human, and eventually power muscle movement or even poetry — but it remains energy. Because of this, energy flows can be measured, optimized, and compared in the way that describes what we identified as technological progress.

But morality is *not* fungible. There is no such thing as a moral unit of measurement. It is not a thing that can pass through contexts unchanged, to be balanced or traded. Yet this is exactly the mistake many societies make, confusing technological progress with moral worth. Energy's fungibility facilitates technical evaluations, but it tells us nothing about which goals we "ought" to pursue. This confusion perpetuates the dangerous fallacy that efficiency and innovation inherently carry ethical value, overlooking the deeper, unquantifiable questions of purpose and integrity. When one tribe has developed a more energy-efficient way to transport wheat, for example, it's tempting for its members to believe this superiority reflects deeper virtue, more "evolved" minds, or even divine favor. History is littered with such beliefs. "God is on our side" has often been little more than "our tools are better."

And this same mistaken logic pervades personal ethics. Helping an elderly man cross the street does not erase the fact that you cheated on your math test four times in Mrs. Shortell's Eighth Grade class. Does volunteering at a soup kitchen on Thanksgiving "make up for" the time when you stole from the cash register at summer camp? Does giving charity to a food bank nullify the moral weight of voting for a candidate who perpetuates an exploitative system? Yet modern moral discourse constantly falls into this trap, treating good deeds as interchangeable with bad ones on an invisible scoreboard.

Where does this instinct come from? Certainly, it mirrors the transactional logic of neoliberal systems, where everything has a price, and value is understood through exchange, but it is far older and more persistent than modern capitalism.

In Catholicism, the practice of confession began to formalize in the early medieval period, with Irish monks introducing penitential books in the 6th and 7th centuries. These manuals prescribed specific penances for particular sins: fasting, prayer, or almsgiving became the moral "cost" to balance the spiritual books. You can almost imagine a late-night telemarketing commercial. "Have you stolen a sheep and you are worried about God's wrath? Don't worry, that can be taken care of with one year of fasting on bread and water or giving alms equivalent to the value of the sheep! Did you break Lent by eating meat? Well, not to fret! That can be balanced by reciting 50 psalms. Great deal, right? Just make sure the meat is good! And hey, we have a special running on adultery at the moment. This spicy sin will only cost you seven years of fasting and abstinence! That sounds like a steal to us! Just make sure you really savor the night!" All jokes aside, though those *were* the actual printed exchange rates, this farce jumped directly into our television sets in the 1980s with late-night preachers promising tickets to heaven with purchases of holy water, shipping and handling not included.

Similarly, in Islam, minor sins can be erased through acts of good deeds, such as giving to charity, fasting, or reciting specific prayers. The Quran describes a divine ledger where each deed is recorded, and the balance of good versus bad determines one's eternal fate. This cosmic bookkeeping reflects an enduring human instinct: the longing for a karmic scoreboard, where morality can be as easily tracked as a bank account or credit score, heaven as the reward for anyone maintaining a score above 600.

The ancient Egyptians had a fascinating manifestation of moral ledgerism with the "Weighing of the Heart" ceremony which occurred just after a death. This event depicted the deceased's heart being weighed against the Feather of Ma'at, an ostrich feather representing truth, justice, and cosmic balance. If the heart was lighter or equal in weight to the feather, the soul was deemed pure and granted entry to the Field of Reeds, a paradisiacal afterlife. However, if the heart was heavier, burdened by deceit or wrongdoing, it was handed over to Ammit — a fearsome hybrid creature with the head of a crocodile, the torso of a lion, and the hindquarters of a hippopotamus — to be devoured. This annihilation symbolized eternal obliteration, a fate *worse* than exclusion from paradise.

The Feather of Ma'at also played a role in Egyptian society. Judges and officials often incorporated the feather into their attire as a visible marker of their commitment to fairness and truth. High-ranking judges, for instance, might wear pendants or headdresses adorned with the feather, signifying their duty to uphold Ma'at's principles in their rulings. Even Pharaohs, considered earthly guarantors of Ma'at, invoked the feather to emphasize their role in maintaining order and justice within the kingdom. The feather on a judge's head might also signal to the community their equivalent "fear" of God and being beholden to a deeper authority. This should all sound perfectly familiar to seeing crosses or other religious symbols adorning the courtrooms all over the world today.

In Zoroastrianism, the soul crosses the Chinvat Bridge after death. The virtuous find the bridge wide and easy to traverse, while the wicked face a narrow path that threatens to plunge them into an abyss. And in Greek mythology, judges like Minos and Rhadamanthus weigh the lives of the dead to assign them to Elysium or Tartarus.

All these examples reflect that there is a deep human instinct to want to reduce the complexity and ambiguity of moral life into a ledger-like system. And they all emphasize *arrival* at a final destination — heaven, paradise, Elysium, a field of reeds — as the ultimate goal where all of the moral tests end in blissful paradise. Death is the bell in the school classroom which marks the end of the exam. Pencils down. No more torture.

But with my emphasis on moral integrity, they all represent the end of the opportunity to encounter moral problems, and engage with moral freedom. In the Egyptian story for example, the soul is either obliterated or sent to paradise. But in my view, both are entirely "inhumane" the moment they confiscate your moral freedom.

If the condition of "freedom," as defined as the ability to encounter and respond to one's cognitive dissonance and cultivate one's integrity, represents the true opportunity of man, this freedom *does not exist* in the Christian heaven, the Egyptian paradise, the Christian hell, or the Egyptian annihilation, but only here in the "human realm" during the "test." The Muslim edit to the picture was an interesting simultaneous softening and hardening of the Christian picture by ensuring punishment for every sin but an ability to "work it off" in hell before one is granted entry into paradise.

Karma, in its original Vedic form, also began as a ritual system of cosmic cause and effect. Over time it evolved into a moral accounting mechanism governing one's next life. Modern New Age versions, like *The Secret*, have turned it into a self-help fantasy. Think good thoughts, and good will come to you. But again, the underlying appeal is the same. We long to make morality measurable and transactional.

In rejecting the karma bank, we are left with a more honest and less stressful and less absurd moral framework. By embracing the singularity and fleeting nature of moral opportunities, we can move beyond the false comfort of moral bookkeeping and toward a deeper understanding of what it means to live with integrity.

Lincoln's Legacy and the Dakota 38

When Americans think of Abraham Lincoln, most remember the man who freed the slaves. The Emancipation Proclamation stands as a monumental moral act, an example of leadership on the "right side of history." It was, by almost universal agreement, the moral issue of his day, and Lincoln passed that test in a way that still resonates.

But that is not the whole story. Lincoln was also the president who authorized the largest mass execution in American history.

In 1862, after a brief but intense conflict known as the US-Dakota War, 303 Native Dakota men were sentenced to death by military tribunals of questionable fairness. Lincoln personally reviewed the cases and reduced the list but still allowed 38 men to be hanged in a public execution in Mankato, Minnesota. The spectacle was horrific. The root causes of the war were clear: broken US promises, massive government corruption, relentless land confiscation and harassment, and engineered starvation among the Dakota people. Yet Lincoln did not stop the hangings. He faced enormous political pressure from white settlers and members of Congress to deliver punishment, and he chose to satisfy them. Perhaps, weighing their continued support as necessary to end Southern slavery.

But Lincoln also held views about Native Americans that many today would find deeply troubling. He described them as "savages" on multiple occasions and spoke casually of westward expansion as an inevitable civilizing mission, one that left little room for Indigenous rights or sovereignty.

I am not offering these facts to condemn Lincoln outright, nor suggest that his statue should probably watch its back, nor to erase any potential moral courage he showed in facing slavery. I am asking us to practice a more mature moral evaluation of any figure, including one as lionized as Lincoln, and allow him to evaluate and live with himself. He, too, faced the dilemmas I am describing. He had to ask himself whether he truly had "no choice" in authorizing those executions, or in allowing certain policies to persist in the name of some "greater good." He had his own cultural constraints and psychological blind spots. He also had, I imagine, a grandmother of some kind offering animals on platters. And he certainly did not have almond milk and tofu in every shop, as I do. The moral opportunities that presented themselves to Lincoln were contextual and situational, as they are for all of us.

If that sounds complicated, it is. And if your takeaway is that, on balance, Lincoln seems to have gotten the *biggest moral question of his time* mostly right, fine. That matters. But then, I would ask you to look around your world, here in the 21st century, or whenever and wherever you happen to be reading this, and ask yourself how you are responding to the great cognitive dissonance of your time. And don't be tempted to think that passing one great test, or aligning yourself with one great cause, tells the whole story of your moral integrity. It is worth much more than that and the quest of moral integrity is much longer than one defining moment.

From Obligation to Opportunity

I want to make a pitch for morality coming from the *inside out*. When I hear people use the language of having a "moral obligation" I hear the suggestions of some kind of external force, whether societal expectations, religious rules, a kind of self-evident imperative, or guilt. I get this feeling and expression. But I don't like it.

"Obligation" implies compulsion, as if morality presses down upon us, dictating our actions. It is, at its core, a consequentialist assumption, another way of saying, "I had no choice" or "I was compelled to act." This framing encourages behavior driven more by pressure than by freedom.

But if we reframe morality not as a doctrine of obligations but as a disconnected sequence of opportunities, we grant ourselves agency and choice, and foster alignment with our values instead of submission to external demands. This subtle shift moves ethics away from coercion and into a space of exploration, where every choice is a deliberate act of self-cultivation.

Integrity is not enforced but built. It is a lifelong process of aligning actions with values with reflection of second order desires and knowledge seeking. And this task remains unchanged, no matter the scale of the problems we face.

Consider animal ethics again. The conventional vegan argument often invokes obligation. "We *must* reduce suffering and eliminate harm." This utilitarian framing also implies a deontological moral command.

Now, imagine two people performing a nearly identical act. One prepares to bring an axe down on a living goat's neck. Its eyes are wide, its body struggling. Its oddly human-like voice straining a cry. The other person is doing the same, but to a highly advanced robotic goat that *perfectly* mimics goat behavior and appearance. It's making all the same cries and moves and eye movements. If you blinked and the two goats were switched you would have no idea.

A pure reduce-suffering-obligation-based utilitarian analysis would have little to say about the robo-goat case, as no actual conscious suffering is occurring. But a moral-integrity-opportunity-based ethics shifts focus to the individual's internal relationship to the act itself. What does *this* action say about their integrity and their engagement with their existential orientation? Ethics, viewed this way, asks us to reflect not only on outcomes but also on the meaning our choices hold within our own personal framework.

Reframing ethics as *opportunity* encourages deeper questioning. How do my choices reflect my deeper sense of self? Instead of acting out of guilt or obligatory compulsion to "save the animals," the individual is invited to cultivate alignment with values like compassion and justice — not under external threat but through intentional choice. I trust the reader can appreciate how this moral consideration lays over the many popular culture depictions of human-like AI robot systems on shows like *Westworld* where it can be quite uncomfortable to watch a human "abuse" and perform all kinds of perverse actions to the nonhuman non-conscious "hosts." This flipping of moral obligation to moral opportunity will also apply to the disturbingly real phenomenon of AI generated pornography.

The obligation-based utilitarian may object here and insist that those cases still fall within the purview since the user of something like AI generated pornography or robot-abusing cowboys are doing a kind of harm to themselves and increasing their *own* suffering. In this way, the language of obligation can be rescued and rephrased as having an obligation *to oneself*, and an obligation to a "better self." To me, this is saying the same thing. That is the opportunity of moral freedom.

This perspective of stressing opportunity not only makes moral responsibility feel more personal and actionable, but it also avoids the paralysis that often comes with overwhelming demands. When ethics is framed as *opportunity* rather than *obligation*, people are more likely to make authentic, sustainable changes. Instead of ticking boxes on an obligatory moral checklist, they can increase their integrity and capacity.

The Museum of Moral Numbness

Writing this book is a privilege, one I feel acutely as I sit here in Madrid's grand research library. The names carved in gold above the marble frieze — R.JIM DERADA, FRAN SUAREZ, QUINTANA — are names I glanced at in Chapter 1. I've since looked them up. Like all of us, these men were complex, morally mixed bags, likely much more so than Abraham Lincoln. If you consider slavery, Spanish imperialism, and colonial conquest to be the "moral issues of their times" then it seems none of them "rose superior." Yet their names gleam here in imperial splendor, a constant reminder that historical injustice can deliver absolutely stunning and seductive architecture which certainly still feels divinely ordained.

Adjoining this building is the National Archaeological Museum. Its polished marble floors click softly beneath my steps as I enter. Each wing is laid out with the confident rhythm of a great European cultural institution. There's a temporary exhibit on Ancient Greece. Something called "Chaos and Cosmos." The irony of that pairing is not lost on me.

I walk with moral eyes, trying on the framing of ethics not as obligation, but opportunity. These little figures behind the glass — clay figurines, worn tools, ceremonial masks — belonged to people as human as we are. The moral differences between us stem not from some deeper essence, but from the relationship they had to the knowledge available to them, and the knowledge they sought. I imagine their own struggles: How do I be good? Am I rationalizing this nagging guilt? Am I brave enough to face what I know?

It's tempting to pity them, to wish I could offer knowledge they lacked. But I know better. This is an infinite regress. Someday a future museumgoer may look at my world and wish they could offer me what they now possess. And I might gladly accept it — clean energy, an end to industrial animal farming, more just economic systems. But none of that would erase the core moral work I must still do. The encounter with cognitive dissonance is eternal.

I imagine Festinger's pegboard experiment unfolding inside one of these little dioramas of ancient peoples. Here, among the huts and clay vessels, he appears with a clipboard, offering tokens to bewildered villagers. The experiment works the same way. Those people knew that lying to their friend was wrong. The absurdity of it only sharpens the point: while technologies shift, the mental gymnastics, the quiet negotiations of integrity, remain eerily constant.

I stop at a display about 19th-century Fijian cannibalism. It would be easy to recoil, to condemn. But I remind myself — their world was governed by knowledge and pressures I cannot fully fathom. Yet I am not off the hook. If morality is about meeting one's own dissonance honestly, I must admit the justifications I still make in my life today.

Of course, I condemn cannibalism. Of course, I think sacrificing children to weather gods is a horrific moral failure. The cowardice and conformity required for such acts must have generated enormous dissonance — or, more chillingly, none at all.

And this forces me to ask — what *can* I truly judge? The people themselves? No. They are too familiar, too much like me. But the systems that failed to foster honest moral reckoning? Those I *can* call immoral. Still, even that judgment is complicated. The historians who curate these exhibits are human too, susceptible to their own moral lures. The urge to frame the past as barbaric and ourselves as enlightened is itself a cognitive dissonance maneuver. Moral progress narratives serve comfort more than truth.

As I exit the museum, I step into modern Madrid. The empire's grandeur remains, now dressed in neon. A massive billboard for breast augmentation looms above a diesel-choked bus. A man walks by eating a cheeseburger from a cow, scrolling on a smartphone built with cobalt mined in Congo. Around me, people swipe through airbrushed social feeds rapidly filling up with morally ambiguous AI generated images, each balancing their own compromises and struggling, I hope, with the constant fight between comfort and conscience.

In a flash, the street becomes a diorama in my mind. I see myself as a tiny figure in this scene. Above me, I imagine a future observer gazing down through museum glass, reading a plaque: "21st Century Consumerism and Environmental Collapse." He sees me, the man typing away on his laptop, trying to sort through these contradictions. I wonder, "Does he know that I saw them too? That I tried to confront them, if imperfectly? Does he know he is not immune, either?"

And this, I think, is the right frame: to see the past, the present, and even the future not through a lens of condemnation or superiority about which obligations we did or did not meet, but as shared terrain of moral opportunity. The encounter with integrity is timeless. The question is always the same: Will we face it honestly? And yes, certain times, certain cultures, certain peoples face it far more or less honestly than others.

So, consider a small field trip. There is almost certainly a museum nearby. One you've been meaning to visit. Let this be your excuse. Go and wander. Look at the faces, the fingertips, the objects that strike you. The moral practices that make you shudder and the ones that make you wonder. Notice your reactions. Make it human, because it was.

And this might be a good time for it. Because you may be wondering, if I reject moral obligation, then where do I claim that morality comes from? To answer that, we'll need to wade into the deep waters of existentialism and meaning-making. But first, stretch your legs. Museum gift shops always have the best stuff. When you're ready, I'll see you in Chapter 8.

Chapter 8

Free Will and the Beautiful Torture of Seeking

How playing the only game in town can rescue us from the doldrums of a mechanistic existence

Responsibility and Freedom: The Architect's Paradox

One lazy Sunday afternoon in Mexico City, my wife and I were on a stroll in the Roma Norte neighborhood. We wandered into a stylish boutique design office where we quickly struck up a conversation with a man, an unmistakably French one. It was his shop, or office, or house, or all three. He was an architect who had been living in Mexico for some time. He made his way onto some covers of snooty architecture magazines by building some flamboyant structures of varying degrees of artistic success. I rather liked some of his work, though that isn't the point of this story.

He was stuffing a hand rolled cigarette between his fingers as we conversed and he leafed through his portfolio, or rather he let me have the honor of the leafing. He was guiding me through his latest project, a striking, almost arrogant piece of modern architecture. I half-listened as he gestured to the structure, explaining the choices he made, the principles he adhered to, the constraints he defied. And when his words (he was talking mostly to an audience of himself by this point) drifted into the relationship of control and ownership over his projects, I caught a phrase that hit my mind like a baseball to the forehead:

> ***"I want responsibility. I want freedom."*** *(It's even more fun to hear this in a thick French accent.)*

He continued with his magazine fodder speech, not even stopping to take credit for the perfection of that phrase. My mind stayed with those words long after he had wandered to the sidewalk to start to drag on that perfectly rolled cigarette.

Freedom and responsibility.

At first, the phrase seems paradoxical. Don't we typically think of *responsibility* as the weight that limits freedom? The obligations that tether us, the commitments that confine us, the duties that close doors rather than open them? When you are a kid you're constantly told that you have "responsibilities" and you must "do your homework" or "study for that exam" or "clean up your room." Don't we have this feeling that those very things are the antithesis of the "freedom of summer break" perhaps? We long for the day that we'll finally move out of the house, and we have ... freedom. Aren't responsibilities the enemy of freedom?

And yet, he said it as if the two are one and the same, as if they exist in some fundamental harmony. And I think they do. Either thing in isolation ceases to be itself. Freedom is the condition for responsibility; responsibility is the price of freedom. The two swiveled in a yin-yang like dance in my mind.

The architect's paradox, of course, is about something more than daring to cantilever a balcony and taking responsibility for either its beauty, its artistic failure, or its deadly collapse. Of course, those are the tangible stakes of *his* profession, but what he was getting at, inadvertently (I was sure of that by the time he rolled his second cigarette), was something deeper, something fundamental to the human condition that surfaces the question of what part of the analogy holds with the general "profession of man."

The phrase, at its core, is a statement about *free will* and human nature.

Is Man Responsible for Himself?

In the realm of philosophy, the debate over the reality of free will often pits incoherent free will determinists against uncaused libertarian free will defenders. On one side, there are thinkers like Sam Harris, Robert Sapolsky, and Gregg Caruso, who argue that free will is an illusion, that our choices are entirely dictated by prior causes beyond our control. They emphasize the mechanical nature of the universe, the physics, the neurobiology, the unseen influences that shape every thought and action. In their view, genuine moral responsibility is something we *think* we have, but it is merely a trick of consciousness, a story our minds tell us to maintain coherence.

And yet, standing next to that architect in Mexico City, it's impossible to imagine he was someone who digested "responsibility" as an illusion. Or if he was, he was staking an impossible but necessary claim to his responsibility, demanding it, because in his mind, it was the *source* of his freedom. (Again, I'm giving the guy too much credit. By now, he was surely off flirting with one of the American spring breakers speaking terrible high-school Spanish and holding an overpriced mango.)

But I suspect this is what so many determinists misunderstand about the human *desire* for free will. It is not merely the ability to make choices. It is the ability to *own* them, to wrestle with them, to take them on as burdens rather than mere inevitabilities.

The paradox of responsibility and freedom is not new. It echoes the writings of existentialists like Jean-Paul Sartre, who famously said that we are "condemned to be free." Sartre understood that radical freedom is not a lightness but a weight. The absence of imposed meaning does not liberate us but instead forces us to create our own. And that creation is, inevitably, an act of moral responsibility.

But, all of that being said, wanting something to be real does not actually make it real. I do take the anti-free will determinist positions seriously. And as this chapter unfolds, we will take the architect's paradox and stretch it further, using it to navigate the dense terrain of free will, determinism, and the way we construct meaning in a world that so often tempts us with escape routes from responsibility.

This is the chapter where I finally confront the probing inquiries of my most philosophically rigorous readers, those who might suspect that I wish to avoid what is known as "the grounding problem." Simply put, this is the challenge of truly grounding any moral claim in something deeper, something more solid than mere "subjective opinion" or "feeling."

The grounding problem is the same problem children discover around the age of five or six when they realize the endlessly fun trick of asking "Why?" in response to every explanation. The game quickly becomes an infinite regress, one that children delight in watching their parents or teachers squirm through until, inevitably, the adult erupts with, "Because I said so!" Many of the best players of the "why game" go on to earn degrees in philosophy.

But I will play the game with myself in this chapter and see just how deep the infinite regress can go in an honest plunge. Here's my punchline upfront: I concede to the determinists when it comes to their analysis of our predicament. Yes, I see the mechanics, the causality, the inevitabilities, the illusion of self, and the impossibility of the common understanding of "free will." But I refuse to relinquish the quest for moral freedom. Instead, I reclaim it. I resurrect the undeniable moral *opportunity* of existence from within a deterministic universe, where true autonomy paradoxically both cannot and yet must exist.

You Were Always Going to Read This, a Nod to the Determinists

The best argument against free will is one that leaves no doors open. Determinism, in its strongest form, does exactly that. Every thought, action, and impulse you've ever had is, according to determinism, the inevitable result of three potential forces: physical nature, historical experience, or the soul. And you did not ultimately choose any of the three at any point. Sometimes arguments about nature versus nurture are actually arguments about free will. So, you can think of the three options as "Nature," "Nurture," and "Soul." Let's walk through them.

Nature is simple enough. It's the physics of the brain, the chemistry of neurons, the grand equation of the universe unfolding according to immutable laws. Whatever the true picture of nature and its laws or patterns turn out to be, or if they are ever attained, they are not of your choosing. In developmental terms this can be a force like genetics, but with physics we have to take it even further. It is not just that the information in the seed plays a role in determining the exact plant that will grow, it's something more like the physical laws (whether they be mathematical or otherwise) *are* the seed which determines the physical universe at any given moment. Nature is the objective universe with its limits, laws, and commandments either drummed up by accident or by God. It does not matter.

Experience, or nurture, is just as straightforward. It's your upbringing, your traumas, the chance encounters that shaped you, the cultural norms embedded in your psyche. In the plant analogy it is the variables of sunlight or water or soil where you found yourself. Those too, at any given moment, are beyond "your" choosing. You did not choose where you were born, when you were born, when that great or terrible thing happened to you, nor anything which unfolded after.

But what about the soul? If we allow it into the discussion, we must grant it special status. It cannot simply be another outcome of physics or history. It must exist outside of those constraints as some sort of metaphysical magic stuff. The soul, in this framework, is divine, existing beyond and apart from both nature and nurture. It is supposed to be the true gem of freedom, the unchained force capable of choice outside deterministic constraints. It is not contingent upon them. It is somehow ladled into our physical selves by a divine presence.

And yet, there is a problem. If the soul is truly independent, how does it interact with the material world? If it influences the brain, then it must operate within the same physical system as neurons and neurotransmitters, subject to laws of causation. If it does not interact, if it remains untouched and unreachable, then it is irrelevant to our choices. Either way, the freedom it promises dissolves upon inspection.

And the deeper problem for the idea of "soul" saving common notions of free will is that you didn't choose your soul either. God did. If this is the source of true freedom and moral ownership, and you happened to have a "nice" soul, well then lucky you. Others might not be so lucky. Again, there is nowhere to slice this picture where we can insert the uncaused self without generating a hopeless circle in the logic.

So where, exactly, is *free will* supposed to exist? What hidden chamber of the self is making choices ungoverned by any of these forces? The answer, determinists argue, is nowhere. It is an illusion. The feeling of "I could have done otherwise" is just that, a feeling. If we rewound the universe, resetting every atom to its exact prior state, you would make the same choice every time. If you had coffee instead of tea this morning, you would always choose coffee. Not because you wanted to. Not because you were "free" to do so. But because every force acting upon you, biological, historical, physical, divine, and environmental, had already set that decision in stone. Of course, you did *have* the feeling of "wanting" the coffee, but that feeling itself was a product of those forces, none of which "you" chose in the first place.

Some try to invoke quantum mechanics to salvage free will from physics. They gesture at randomness, at the built-in uncertainty, at some unknowable dimension of human choice that exists in the gaps of predictability. But randomness is not free will, it is precisely the opposite. A choice made by chance is still not a choice made by you. A universe with quantum uncertainty still yields a determined outcome, only now it includes unpredictable elements outside of your control. If anything, quantum mechanics merely makes the choice you will make fundamentally *unknowable,* rather than free. That wonderfully weird unknowability may be enough to jumpstart a *conversation* about meaningful moral opportunity, as people like Sean Carroll argue. And personally, I tend to agree.

But in any case, the determinist framework appears airtight. And once accepted, the weight of its implications comes crashing down.

However, most determinists still recognize the necessity of *practical* moral responsibility. They do not argue that, because no one is *truly* responsible for their actions, society should function without consequences. Instead, they adopt what might be called social free will, a framework where people, though not morally responsible in any cosmic sense, are still held accountable as a practical measure.

Consider a grizzly bear. If a hiker wanders into its territory and gets mauled, we do not hold the bear "morally responsible." But if a hungry, agitated bear is prowling around a crowded café at noon, we recognize that something must be done. The bear is a danger, regardless of its lack of intent or agency. If we had the means, we might tranquilize it rather than kill it because we recognize that it is unlucky to have been born a bear, with its instincts and hunger.

Extend this analogy to people. If human beings, like bears, are just physical systems running on biological programming and environmental influence, does this not also make them unlucky to be the way they are? This realization leads many determinists toward a moral framework of compassion rather than retribution. Instead of punishment for its own sake, they argue for intervention, rehabilitation, and solutions that acknowledge human behavior as an inevitable outcome rather than a choice.

I hope I have done the determinists proud in representing their view fairly. I do not find logical mistakes in their scientific arguments. I do not even find their conclusions irrational. But, importantly, what I *do* find is a massively psychologically appealing thesis, one that provides relief from the tortures of moral freedom and responsibility and the existential burden of pride or shame. And in that massive appeal to *Escape From*

Freedom as Erich Fromm warned, I find their attack on free will to be deeply troubling, while I accept their primary arguments.

This is where the determinists and I usually part ways in our conversations.

It starts as a little nudge but ends with our trajectories being light years apart on important political and moral questions, like two asteroids who were once neighbors before one was ticked by a small drifting stone in the deterministic cosmos.

From God to Gravity: The Escape Hatch of Free Will Denial

The anti-free will determinists tend to be quite hostile to religious philosophies which emphasize cosmic punishments for sin. I think the reasons should be obvious. The circular logic of the nature, nurture, soul trinity results in God dishing out reward or punishment for the type of soul which he or she ladled into you. I think the Christian presentation of the trinity somewhat mirrors this predicament with the Son (nature and flesh?), Father (nurture and guidance?), and Holy Spirit (free will soul stuff?). Although, no one seems to be able to really figure out precisely what is going on there. Certain denominations like the Calvinists seemed to admit defeat to the determinists as well, but perversely contended that Earthly rewards and punishments or ailments were merely hints at whether your soul was destined for Heaven or Hell. And there was really nothing you could do about it except watch the play unfold.

The rug is pulled out from many of the Abrahamic religious stories in this deterministic analysis. I'm fully on board with that move. But oftentimes the anti-free will determinists end up replacing God with physics.

They take the perverse moral obedience to God and exchange it for cold, neutral causality and inescapable obedience to physics.

This is not to say that determinists abandon ethics, most don't. But what they do abandon is the crushing existential burden of believing that their every action, every regret, every failure was their own in a deeply meaningful and mysterious sense.

So, in this way, determinism becomes one of the most powerful tools in the Cognitive Dissonance Repairman's kit. Just think about how strong the thing is. "If you took the $1 dollar from Festinger and lied to the perfectly innocent awaiting students, don't worry, the entire decision was set in motion for you long ago! You see all those gears turning that say that you lied for a buck? No need to fret or feel shame! There are actually gears all over the entire universe and the whole thing is unfolding according to rules and laws or divine accidents that really can't be pinned on you. You are all good! In fact, 'you' don't really even exist! 'You' as a self-authoring thing are just an illusion and product of the mechanical universe!"

Determinism, for all its scientific rigor, offers something deeply seductive: the erasure of guilt, the dissolution of personal failure. And it comes wrapped in an intellectual package that doesn't require you to profess belief in resurrection or miracles or divine favor.

Zen and the Art of Dissonance Repair

This desire to be free from freedom finds further validation in another domain: deep meditation practices, particularly those rooted in Buddhist traditions. Many deterministic thinkers engage with these disciplines, drawn by the idea that free will is an illusion best understood through direct experiential insight. The practice of breaking the identification between thinker and thought, recognizing that thoughts simply arise, unbidden, can be a profound and liberating realization. Many who meditate experience this as a form of psychological relief, a step toward harmony with the universe.

I do not deny or doubt the truth of this effort, nor its benefits. I have glimpsed these states myself, in meditation and in altered states of mind. Recognizing the self to be an illusory vantage point rather than an agent, while potentially insightful and calming, also raises deeper questions about engagement, agency, and the nature of meaning in a deterministic universe.

And this is my big bone to pick with determinists of any stripe. While they have successfully dismantled the idea of cosmic responsibility, they have done absolutely no work toward solving "the grounding problem" which I introduced in Chapter 3, which is concerned with trying to find an ultimate objective foundation for moral truths.

So, what does it mean to say something is a "moral danger" in a deterministic world? I have deliberately used that word in this chapter, referencing grizzly bears and "dangerous" humans, but without justification. But what is that word "danger" doing, other than injecting a moral urgency and assumed desired outcome?

The most common response among determinists seems to be a claim that a danger is anything that threatens the universe's capacity to produce conscious flourishing in the future. In other words, a suicide bomber walking into a café is a danger because their action disrupts the deterministic universe's ability to perpetuate well-being. But again, this response inserts "flourishing" without defining or carefully considering it.

Determinists, once they erase true free will, tend to adopt an unexamined scientism, a naive and incoherent utilitarianism that takes over like an occupying force, making claims about "better" and "worse" without any grounding for why those concepts hold weight, while attempting to quantify and measure all of the "flourishing" outputs of the universe. For example, without reopening our previous chapters too deeply, I did not tell you the *reason* for that suicide bomber in the café. I do not know exactly how to evaluate how much "flourishing" or "suffering" is added or subtracted if that person was historically and morally framed as a "freedom fighter" in Algeria, South Africa, Peru, or was Nat Turner himself fighting against slavery. And deterministic utilitarians don't know how to measure it either.

The problems are these: Why should the universe persist? Why should it thrive? Why should suffering be minimized? The deterministic worldview assumes these goals are self-evident and self-answering. And once the self has been dissolved, once the thinker has successfully separated from the thought, once moral responsibility has been erased, what remains is an empty assumption: that the universe *ought* to continue so that self-defining well-being can increase. But why? The determinist, defaulting into utilitarianism, has no answer other than appealing to the goodness of goodness itself, in a silly and self-defeating argument.

This is why I find the psychological appeal of determinism so fascinating. It offers the dissolution of self, the erasure of personal guilt, and the escape from the exhausting burden of choice. And yet, for all its intellectual rigor, it remains mute on the fundamental question: why any of this should matter at all?

Maybe you think I'm just confused. That "goodness" is simply self-evident. That I've talked myself into a corner of moral madness, unable to articulate any moral attitude beyond fashion or preference. I hope the "opportunity over obligation" arguments from the previous chapter earn me a bit of charity and help clarify that I'm not pretending to stand on solid ground so much as admitting the cheat that lets me walk forward anyway. Still, I've heard intelligent thinkers I admire dismiss these kinds of questions as mere confusion.

For example, at a debate I attended, both Carlo Rovelli and Slavoj Žižek scoffed at David Chalmers' famous formulation of what he called *The Hard Problem of Consciousness*. I've heard the problem posed in many ways, but at its core, it asks: why physical processes don't just function, but also come with *experience*? Why does the universe bother with impotent subjectivity? Why should anything that happens *happen to someone*?

I admit that I am not satisfied with proclamations of, "It just works like that!" Maybe this is just my younger self, still stuck playing the annoying "why" game and protesting my cosmic parent who is shouting, "Because I said so!" from the driver's seat. That familiar standoff even comes with its old bribes: *"Stop asking why and we'll get ice cream on the way home. You like ice cream, don't you?"* Which, in philosophical terms, becomes: *"Why are you asking why the universe includes you? It feels good sometimes, doesn't it? Isn't that enough? Aren't you having a good time?"*

No. I want to know why I exist. Sue me.

I've never been satisfied with those answers or taken those bribes, and that really may be foolish. It may be a recipe for personal disaster. People like Jordan Peterson certainly think that it is. Being preoccupied with these questions might be a formula for madness. The expulsion from the Garden of Eden seems, in a way, to reflect that very lesson. I've always imagined Adam biting the apple and suddenly asking Chalmers' hard question. "Wait, why did that *taste* like *anything*?" God must have rolled his eyes and banished him for his own good.

But there's always been something comforting in those stories. I think, "At least I'm not alone! I'm not the only one bothered by this stuff! And why did you put the damn apple there in the first place?! You wanted me to learn obedience and not ask why I was in a garden forever?!"

Anyway, to explore this predicament more deeply, let's take a detour into one of the greatest illustrations of this clash between the philosophical erasure of free will and the simultaneous psychological desire for it, from the brilliant mind of Rod Serling and *The Twilight Zone.*

A Too Perfect Break, a Too Imperfect Miss

A Nice Place to Visit, written by Charles Beaumont, is one of the best episodes of *The Twilight Zone* among a catalog of gold. Obvious spoiler alert here.

The episode opens with Rocky Valentine, a small-time crook and gambler, fleeing from a botched robbery on a dark street. The offscreen cops are firing their guns in pursuit and eventually strike him. He crumbles to the ground. Out.

Upon regaining consciousness, he finds himself in an alley. There, he meets a genial, white-suited man named Pip, who introduces himself as Rocky's guide, tasked with providing him whatever he desires. Skeptical and wary, Rocky suspects a setup and, upon being led to a luxurious apartment, demands to know the catch. Pip assures him there is none, but Rocky remains distrustful. When presented with a lavish meal, Rocky insists Pip taste it first, fearing it might be poisoned. Pip claims he has forgotten how to eat, prompting Rocky to shoot him at close range only to watch in disbelief as the bullets have no effect. It's then that Rocky begins to suspect something supernatural is at play, and that Pip might be an angel and this is the afterlife.

Pip alerts him to the phone where he can be reached and he leaves Rocky to his luck.

The apartment is lavish. The food is fantastic. The clothes fit him perfectly. Rocky is thrilled. At first, Rocky revels in the endless luxury. He wins every bet at the casino, every wish is fulfilled, women are draped over his arm, and he's treated like royalty.

But as time passes, frustration seeps in. Whatever he wants happens exactly as he envisions. So what's the problem?

One night, after shooing three preening women out of his apartment, he picks up a pool cue and takes a hasty break shot. Every ball finds a pocket in perfect, uncanny precision. But instead of joy, unease washes over him. He calls Pip. He appears instantly.

Something is wrong. He's winning *too* much. Everything unfolds *exactly* as he wills it. Pip offers a solution: he can introduce some uncertainty, perhaps make Rocky miss now and then? Rocky is into the idea for a moment, but even simpleton Rocky can figure this one out. "That's no good. I'll *know* you're doing it." If he misses, it won't be because of skill, failure, or chance, it will be because Pip (or a random quantum roll of the dice) decided it was time for a miss.

Panic sets in. Rocky starts questioning the nature of this afterlife. How could this possibly be heaven? As doubt consumes him, Pip's pleasant demeanor shifts into something more sinister. He grins. "Heaven? Who told you this was *heaven*?" The realization crashes down on Rocky. This is *the other place.* Cue the maniacal laughter and the classic *Twilight Zone* score as the camera pulls away, leaving Rocky trapped in an existence where every desire is fulfilled except the one that truly matters: the ability to doubt, to struggle, to reenter the mystery of free will. In other words, the very state he was in before the gunshot.

Beaumont's script brilliantly flips the idea of paradise on its head. Rocky's torment isn't punishment in the traditional sense; it is the unbearable monotony of a world without genuine struggle or mystery. If one pays close attention, the episode reveals the true horror of "meeting God." For what is Pip, if not Rocky's God?

If Rocky could have one wish in this anti-paradise, it would be for Pip to erase his memory of ever having met him, to never know for certain whether Pip exists, to be thrust back into the uncertainty of life before the bullet hit him. That would be true rebirth, the only paradise that makes sense is a world of endless questions, of struggle, of grappling with the fundamentally unknown and wanting to know what we shouldn't. We don't *want* God in our world. We want to be the creators of our choices, even if the determinists have recognized the logical flaw in that thinking.

This is the true position of atheistic humanism as best as I can unveil it. A position which does not *reject* God per say, but resents the suggestion that actually finding God would be of any importance to us while the endless search for the nature of God and man is the task at hand. It is a sort of reverse Garden of Eden where we would never want to return to such a place of impotence and unexamined obedience.

The human spirit, as *A Nice Place to Visit* suggests, does not thrive in ease alone. Without the possibility of moral failure, without real moral stakes, existence is mechanical, robotic, and torturous no matter how blissful and peaceful.

Which brings us to the real question of, what separates mere existence from the pursuit of something greater? It's not struggle alone that gives life meaning, it's our confrontation with our capacity for counterfactual moral world creation: the ability to imagine how things ought to be and to take that tension seriously. Rocky never showed much interest in doing that before the gunshot. But now? He'd give anything to go back and get another stab at it, to wrestle with failure, doubt, and cognitive dissonance, rather than endure this endless loop of peace, sex, and success. Gross.

That brings us directly to the grounding problem which I've been tiptoeing towards. This is my attempt to get "almost grounded" in moral meaning. But before we go there, one last tip of the toe, a quick note on a very common and frightening escape hatch from the burden of freedom.

A Note on Cults, Nationalism, and Mobs

When I interviewed Benjamin Storey about his book *Why We Are Restless* — which follows four French philosophers grappling with the same core idea raised by the French architect at the start of this chapter, that deep restlessness born from simultaneously desiring and fearing moral freedom — he pointed to Rousseau as a key figure. Rousseau, he noted, offered a kind of relief from this burden by urging individuals to dissolve themselves into the greater cause of the nation.

Storey and I were discussing the powerful draw of cults, armies, and nationalist movements. I asked him why people so readily surrender their individuality to such groups. His answer was simple, and perfect: "It is *because* the individual is erased that these groups will always be so attractive."

There is comfort and relief in surrendering the moral self to something vast, something inevitable, something with marching orders, quite literally. People join armies not just for the cause, but for the erasure of individual burden. They succumb to religious fervor not just for salvation, but for the relief of responsibility.

Rousseau, you can imagine, is often tapped as a favorite philosopher of ethno-nationalist supremacist groups. Though it would be unfair to cast his entire body of work into that bucket.

One might respond to all this by insisting that "freedom comes through discipline." And that phrase, while not entirely wrong, is often a disguised appeal for the relief of not having to choose. I don't scoff at the appeal of discipline. Many people turn to it as a way to rein in their more unruly impulses, and that's valid. Structure can help us focus, reset, and reclaim a sense of direction. But in my effort to shift the entire moral conversation from obligations to opportunities, I'd offer a caution. Discipline can easily drift into obedience. And when it does, it stops shaping the self and starts erasing it just as determinists and religious ideologues often do.

If this next section lands for you, then you'll recognize that true moral freedom doesn't avoid discipline, it demands it. But not the kind that silences you or yells at you to tuck in the corners of an army cot. It's the kind that allows you to attend to your moral confidence in an indifferent world.

Almost Grounded, Sagan's Invitation

Where does morality come from?

Every book on moral philosophy asks this question. And most of us twist ourselves in knots trying to answer it. Evolutionary psychologists often point to biology, explaining our moral feelings as adaptations for survival. These are useful explanations for why we might feel certain things. But they don't offer real grounding. Eventually, they fall into the trap of assuming that because something exists in nature, it must be good. That's the naturalistic fallacy. You can describe a law of nature, but that doesn't mean you shouldn't imagine a world with a morally better one. This kind of evolutionary angle seems to work just fine for explaining why people might find incest morally repulsive, for example. It does damage to the gene pool when family members reproduce. Groups survive better when child rearing is shared amongst strangers. And so on. These kinds of moral behaviors might have evolved due to their "prosocial" nature.

But in the end, it always circles back to the same goal, keep the species going. Survival for its own sake is the prime directive of evolution.

Preachers answer differently. Morality comes from God. That's the foundation. Whether we can *understand* God is debated. But there's no question, in their view, that God knows what's right and wrong.

David Hume figured this out for us. Depressingly. He was the philosopher who first admitted defeat to the grounding problem when he said, "There is no description of the way the universe is that tells us how the universe ought to be." Sometimes, this is called "the is-ought" problem.

I want Hume to be wrong.

But he wasn't.

Now, some people take this too far and conclude that all morality is subjective. They drive a wedge between scientific facts and moral opinions and declare that the two shall never meet. This position can land you in some morally ridiculous ground where you feel like you have to consider all moral opinions as equally valid and fair. The worst application of this would be absolute cultural moral relativism. This plagues some political philosophical conversations where people refuse to pass judgment on something like human sacrifice.

But others slam too hard in the other direction and treat facts as moral truths in disguise. That's where utilitarianism usually goes wrong, and I've said plenty about that already.

So, what's left? Well, here is how I answer the grounding problem and respond to David Hume's challenge.

There is one particular fact, one description of how the universe is which gets me as close to an *ought* from an *is* as I think is possible. And it comes from Carl Sagan. He once observed, "We are a way for the universe to know itself."

It sounds like poetry but it is an objective observation. There's no claim about *why* we have this ability. Just the recognition of the mystery that we do.

And yes, Hume is still right. There is nothing in Sagan's observation that tells me that the universe *ought* to know itself. But it sure seems like that is the only game in town. The only real alternative is to walk away. To stop participating. Suicide, in the literal sense, but also in the deeper sense I've been circling throughout the book. Whether it's rules, results, or dreaming of being a bird, these are all versions of shutting the door. Each one turns away from the strange opportunity of being a self-aware piece of this universe. It is the rejection of what I call *Sagan's Invitation*.

But, you *can* forego it. You do not have an *obligation* to stay alive and engage with the universe's ability to be known by itself. I don't really have a problem with suicide as such. But I feel the sting of it as the evidence of a missed *opportunity*. Survival is a prerequisite to accept the invitation, but that is all it is worth. Survival for its own sake (as evolution promotes) is an *amoral* action. And it follows that I think ending someone else's survival against their will is an *immoral* act. But this is the key distinction. The opposite of *immoral* is not *moral*, it can simply be amoral.

This, for me, is as close as I can get to grounding. It doesn't give me a single rule, but it offers a place to jumpstart the conversation. I don't know if the universe *wants* to be known. But I know I am part of it, and I *want* to be known. I want to understand what I am, and what I could have been. And knowing *how* I work mechanically or how the universe works physically is not good enough. There is a deeper sense of *knowing* that I want. I want to know what ought to be and ought to have been. If there is anything to "maximize" in this universe it would be to maximize the capability of the universe to know itself. This deep dive into grounding rescues for me a tangible sense of the sacredness of consciousness which fires up the moral aspect of existence.

The "I" that is inhabited by me, this perspective and collection of sensation which generates my consciousness at this particular moment, is unique and distinct. It is only mine. It is purely subjective and unapproachable by anything other than this inner place. If one pictures the universe and its possible states to be a kind of infinite object and my current view of it to be an infinitesimal window upon it which only I am "being" with all of the infinite potential to know itself that is available, if I become lost, extinguished, erased, or merely squandered, the loss would be irreplaceable and unrecoverable, including the knowledge of the universe which could have been gained.

This is a grand way of proving that every consciousness is precious and every death is an infinite loss.

Another way to underscore the moral emptiness of survival alone, that it only sets the stage for moral self-awareness, is through another classic phrase from moral philosophy, "ought implies can." If you say someone ought to do something, you're assuming they're able to. That idea crashes into the next chapter, which takes up the most common objection to everything I've argued so far. What if your hands are truly tied? What if the world forces you to violate your moral integrity. Even when we *ought* to do something, sometimes we simply *can't*. What then?

Chapter 9

The Politics of Necessity and Purity

When the "I had No Other Choice" defense is strong

The Sweet Escape of "I Had No Choice"

There's something undeniably seductive about being backed into a corner. No one says they want to be there, but once you're in it, moral clarity can emerge like a gift. Suddenly, the complexity evaporates. Your options narrow to a single road, even if it's a rather grim one, and you're allowed, maybe even applauded, for taking it. These situations offer us the relief of being forced to act and assuages our fear of judgment. The ambiguity is replaced with inevitability. You get to say the magic words: "I had no choice."

This is why the classic trolley problem, first posed by Philippa Foot in 1967, still holds such power. The trolley problem has gained a lot of attraction lately so you may know it already. The scenario is simple. A runaway trolley is headed toward five people tied to a track. You're standing by a lever. If you pull it, the trolley will switch to another track where only one person is tied down. Do you pull the lever and actively kill one to save five? Or do nothing and let five die?

This dilemma gave rise to countless variations: the "fat man" version, where you push someone off a bridge to stop the trolley while killing them; the "loop track" variation; scenarios involving loved ones, AI drivers, and more. On the Internet and in ethics classrooms, these scenarios multiply like rabbits, each one tweaking conditions to test where our values bend or break.

The attraction, and perverse "fun," of these trolley games does not need to necessarily be a morally loaded scenario like borderline involuntary manslaughter. It is reflected in psychological studies about general choice paralysis. We often feel more comfortable when the burden of *any* discretion is removed, whether that be moral in nature or of preferred sandwich toppings. Sheena Iyengar's famous, perfectly named, "jam study" is a great example.

In the study, shoppers at a grocery store were presented with a display of 24 varieties of jam, while another group saw only 6.

While more people stopped to sample from the larger selection, far fewer actually made a purchase. The smaller selection led to more buying decisions. This counterintuitive finding helped launch a broader understanding of choice paralysis: the more options we have, the harder it can be to choose and the less satisfied we are with our choices. The study, and those like it, also certainly affected our grocery shelves in nations where we claim to love having infinite free choices.

Strawberry jam and Strawberry-Blackberry-Hint-of-Blueberry jam choices aside, this chapter is about the morally weighty decisions where we are *sure* that choice *is* severely limited or nonexistent. Having no choice is the best friend of the consequentialist, of the utilitarian, and of those of us exhausted by moral ambiguity. So you can confidently guess: I'm not really a fan of this one.

But this chapter isn't a rejection of hard moral situations. It's a serious engagement with them. Philosopher Lisa Tessman has written extensively about these moments in her book *When Doing the Right Thing Is Impossible*. She explores the ethical terrain where every available option leads to harm. One of the most chilling real-world examples comes from Hurricane Katrina, where doctors and nurses in a flooded, powerless hospital had to make unthinkable decisions. They were forced into real-world triage, deciding which patients could be carried up to the roof for rescue, sometimes choosing based on weight to conserve time and strength. Some patients were left behind. And in the most nightmarish cases, Tessman describes how healthcare workers administered lethal injections to certain patients, believing it was the most humane (or least bad) option available, faced with the choice between letting them drown or starve in the dark. In these scenarios, every path is tainted, and Tessman argues that there are no "right" paths to take. Tessman argues that there are moral violations so profound they remain morally wrong, even when they are the best of terrible options.

They aren't "canceled out" by the counterfactual universe that wasn't chosen. You can think of them as something which is so heavy that if you try to put it on the utilitarian scale of maximizing flourishing or minimizing suffering, it simply breaks the scale.

I've always been drawn to this analysis, not just philosophically but psychologically. Imagine a soldier returns from war, haunted by bombing a school to "neutralize" (kill) a target (a human). His commanding officers had said it was a strategic necessity, and it created a horrific result of "collateral damage" (dead, maimed, and mutilated children). Let's say he enters my psychological practice, searching for answers and relief.

I've always thought it would not be very helpful for me to say, "Well, it's alright really. You had no choice. I get that it's hard, but what choice did you have? You did the least bad thing you could in a really tough scenario." What might help much more (and what I think is philosophically true) is saying, "Well, you committed a sacred moral violation. That's why it hurts. That's why you're struggling. Even if your hands were tied, it was still awful and a moral wrong. Nothing will change that unfortunately. So let's talk about how to carry that pain honestly and how we can address the belief that you are a good person."

All of this is the terrain of the classic nightmare scenarios, lifeboat problems, hostage dilemmas, and of course, the trolley problem itself. They're toy universes built to test our limits. And sometimes they echo reality. But there is a glaring problem with things like the trolley problem or even Peter Singer's famous drowning child which was a scenario where you face the decision to run into a muddy shallow pond to save a drowning child but in the process, you'll ruin your new pair of $100 shoes. The point of Singer's seemingly very easy situation is to point out how we are figuratively walking by those ponds all the time in the moments when we forego a donation to a charity which can definitively show that your donation will save the life of a child in Zimbabwe. When we waive them off and purchase a pair of new shoes or 15 awful Starbucks drinks instead, we are effectively letting that child drown. Singer argues that actually seeing and hearing the child in the pond is just a morally arbitrary artifact of proximity which should not be morally decisive.

But the problem with these toy universes is they plunge you into a life and death decision at the very moment of truth as if that is when the world began. In those spots there is no time to stop and ask, "Hey, who built this stupid trolley in the first place? Why wasn't there a fence around the pond? And can we prevent more ponds or trolleys like this from popping up in the future?"

Sure, maybe you *should* rush in and save the kid first and then ask those questions. But we should get around to asking them at some point, right?

This is where my real concern starts to set in. Because my focus here is the psychological pull, the way the "I had no choice" script works as a kind of cognitive dissonance repair tool. It doesn't just describe genuine moral paradoxes. It's become something else entirely, a tool, a secular ideology, a license for violence, evasion, and self-congratulation.

The attraction to the "no choice" defense has grown into a systematized excuse. It generates a massive incentive structure, an open invitation, for opportunism disguised as necessity. We see this clearly in modern geopolitics, where crises become cover stories, and old dreams emerge as urgent needs. After the 9/11 attacks, the Bush administration invoked the rhetoric of moral necessity. Terrorism, they said, left them no choice. But we now know that several members of that same administration had long wanted to invade Iraq and "redraw" the Middle East. The attacks were not the origin of their plans, but the justification for them. The "no choice" refrain became the alibi.

The same script echoed again after October 7th. Following the Hamas attack, Israel launched a campaign of destruction, displacement, domination, genocide, and conquest that had long been dreamed of by significant segments of the Zionists for over 100 years. In the early stages, the dominant language was that of necessity. Israel had "no choice" but to "root out terrorists and eliminate Hamas." But soon, a different tone began to seep into public discourse. Officials and commentators began referring to the assault as a "window of opportunity." It was, as many noted, a case of saying the quiet part out loud — a phrase that perfectly captures the dynamic I'm trying to highlight.

And so the questions must be asked, when the justification is ready *before* the event, how much of the event was just an opportunistic gift? Or worse, how much was encouraged, provoked, or even engineered? These are incendiary questions, and this is not the book to litigate their specific details. I won't use this space to weigh evidence of false flags. And my line of caution is simple for guarding oneself against conspiracy theory mindsets: *just because you've located the beneficiaries of a world event doesn't mean you've necessarily located its architects.* That said, false flag operations happen. They are well-documented tactics in military and intelligence history. So, the real danger is not in asking these questions, but in failing to recognize the seductive shield that the "I had no choice" excuse becomes in moments of high emotion and retaliation. It's nearly bulletproof.

A world full of hard, or supposedly forced, choices is a world primed for shrugs and absolved of moral responsibility. That's why this framework has quietly evolved into a kind of secular ideology. It presents itself as neutral, objective, and rational. But it deserves serious scrutiny. Because once you accept that the world is made of unavoidable trade-offs and lesser evils, it becomes easy to see *every* moral failure as merely unfortunate or tragic but necessary, and retain what you want to call "compassion."

When I was preparing to film an interview with the aforementioned and famously hard-nosed utilitarian Sam Harris, he and I were chatting informally about his moral framework. At one point, with a kind of dry amusement, he said, "It's all trolley problems. All the way down." That line has always stuck with me. It captures the deep ideological commitment to a worldview built entirely out of trade-offs and an endless gauntlet of lesser evils.

And this kind of thinking isn't new to the modern "rationalist" crowd. Take Thomas Jefferson, for example, and his evolving (or devolving) view of Native Americans.

Thomas Jefferson Justifies a Genocide

Jefferson is often tapped as one of the great American rationalists — a founding father who distrusted religious dogma and believed in reason, science, and Enlightenment thought. He famously created his own version of the New Testament, literally cutting out all the miracles and supernatural elements with a razor blade. This impulse echoes, surprisingly, the recent expression by someone like Richard Dawkins, who is far more hostile to religious claims of miracles than Jefferson ever was. In 2024, Dawkins said: "I call myself a cultural Christian. I'm not a believer, but there's a distinction between being a believing Christian and a cultural Christian ... I love hymns and Christmas carols and I sort of feel at home in the Christian ethos." It's become fashionable in certain atheist rationalist circles to espouse this kind of position. Figures like Ayaan Hirsi Ali have echoed the sentiment, writing: "Western civilization is under threat ... Judeo-Christian values offer the best defense of human dignity and individual freedom."

Jefferson, for his part, was a champion of secular government and a man who claimed to build his worldview on evidence and logic. In many ways, he represents the American origin story of a certain kind of "reasonable man, suspicious of fanaticism, committed to progress, and willing to make tough calls in the name of future flourishing."

But there's a trick buried in that posture. Because "reason" and "necessity" are easy allies. And when reason becomes divorced from humility or moral self-interrogation, when it gets laundered through the language of inevitability, it has no real brakes. It becomes a rhetorical instrument for making anything seem justified, even if regrettable. Jefferson's writings about Native Americans, spanning over two decades, offer a masterclass in this kind of drift.

In his 1785 work, *Notes on the State of Virginia,* Jefferson expressed a belief in the inherent equality of Native Americans, stating, "The American Indian is a man in body and mind equal to the white man, and of courage perhaps superior. If we could extinguish the Indian fire in his breast and induce him to labor with us, the world would not contain a more magnificent race of men." The sentiment implies a potential for coexistence, a mix of admiration and condescension. The racism laced into the phrase "Indian fire" is unmistakable, but at least at this stage, Jefferson wasn't calling for their elimination. The trolley, as it were, was still a ways off.

But as the young nation expanded westward — along with the lure of land, wealth, and power — Jefferson's tone began to shift. In a letter to William Henry Harrison dated February 27, 1803, he outlines a strategy to pressure Native Americans into ceding their lands: "In this way our settlements will gradually circumscribe and approach the Indians, and they will in time either incorporate with us as citizens of the United States or remove beyond the Mississippi." The rumbling of the trolley grew louder, the inevitability chugged closer. He continues in the same letter, outlining a strategy of economic coercion, "To promote this disposition to exchange lands ... we shall push our trading houses, and be glad to see the good and influential individuals among them run in debt ... when these debts get beyond what the individuals can pay, they become willing to lop them off by a cession of lands."

By 1813, Jefferson was 70 years old, and his rhetoric had hardened. In a letter to General Andrew Jackson, he writes, "If we are to wage a campaign against these people, the end proposed should be their extermination, or their removal beyond the lakes or Illinois river." In another letter that same year, to Alexander von Humboldt, he writes, "This unfortunate race, whom we had been taking so much pains to save and to civilize, have, by their unexpected desertion and ferocious barbarities, justified extermination."

Time to pull the trolley lever.

The progression, from paternalistic assimilationism to exterminationist logic, all under the guise of reluctant rationalism, is chilling. Especially when framed as the final step in a chain of tragic inevitabilities. This is the logic of someone who believes he has stumbled into a moral bind, one that justifies what would otherwise be unthinkable. It's the logic of the trolley problem, dragged into the real world as a convenient justification for actions driven by expansionist ambitions.

So how are we, today, supposed to evaluate Jefferson's motivations? Are we to believe that he and others were constantly searching for a "forced hand" excuse to expel or kill Native peoples because the land was simply too valuable to ignore? Or do we take him at his word, that he really did believe in their potential, that he really was reluctantly pushed into genocide, step by logical step?

My point is that both are likely true. The first might be true on a sociological level. The incentives of economic promise and the lure of power will become the morally sanitized and more "obvious" real motivation written down by history books, and a religiously laced concept like "manifest destiny" coined about

30 years later by a journalist would settle in as the reinforcing ideology. But Jefferson would have rejected the overtly religious notion that the white man was destined to expand all the way to the Pacific Ocean through God's providence. What were the "genuinely held beliefs" of Mr. Jefferson in the early 1800s? I have no idea, but I would guess that the Repairman in his head had done plenty of work to get him to a place where he consciously believed he had no choice and the Natives had pulled the lever on themselves through their own behavior.

Jefferson's case exemplifies how the veneer of reason can be used to mask moral transgressions. The "I had no choice" defense, when wielded by those in power, can transform from a personal lament into a systemic rationale for oppression. It underscores the danger of allowing purported necessity to override moral integrity consideration. And it should highlight how there is almost always a series of events and moral choices which lead up to the dreaded trolley problem moment where levers of ethnic cleansing, genocide, murder, or worse are pulled.

And it's an evergreen cautionary tale which should sound very familiar today.

The Lure of the "Clash of Civilizations" and Giant Trolley Tracks

This general worldview of "having no choice" is rampant in many of the intellectual circles I used to run in. There was a deep attraction to this way of seeing the world — as a kind of grand tournament of ideas. Competing civilizations, each defined by the beliefs they hold most dear, clashing in some tragic-but-necessary battle to determine whose worldview prevails. It's seductive. It feels clean. It flatters the rational mind, with its veneer of philosophical rigor, as if we're all just dispassionate referees trying to help the "good" ideas win and the "bad" ones fade into history.

If you come from a framework that sees ideas as the drivers of history — belief governs behavior, full stop — then this battlefield logic feels natural. It feels like what grown-ups should be talking about. And it has a kind of internal consistency.

Take a hypothetical cultural practice — say, a community that believes every third child born must be sacrificed to God. In the intellectual circles I moved through, we might all agree that this practice is morally abhorrent. But from there, the conversation would splinter into different frameworks of objection. Some would argue from a utilitarian perspective, weighing harm and consequence. Others might appeal to sacred human dignity, or to the absence of divine mandate. A few might try to understand the metaphysics behind the belief — perhaps even entertain it in an abstract sense. The point, though, was that we were taking the belief at face value. We were accepting that this belief governed the behavior, and then arguing — sometimes intensely — about how best to discredit or override it. That was the model. You evaluate the belief. You bring better beliefs into the ring. You out-argue, out-reason, out-value.

But what was missing from all this was the more destabilizing question: *Is the belief alone really what motivates the behavior?* And even if it is, *how did that belief come to be held so strongly, so widely, that it could organize a culture around it?* We weren't asking how the belief got its power. What history, what trauma, what material incentives or colonial distortions brought it to the surface? We treated belief as a self-contained moral atom — something you could study, isolate, and replace.

And in many of those circles, that's what passed for meaningful political engagement. Heterodox debates. Tediously long podcasts. Heroic intellectual jousting over the moral validity of religious doctrines or liberal democratic ideals. People convincing themselves that this, somehow, is how the future gets built: one argument at a time.

But this entire framework is broken. And dangerously so. Beliefs *don't* float in a vacuum. And moral behavior doesn't erupt from ideas *alone*. That was the blind spot.

Yes, of course beliefs influence behavior. And specific beliefs steer behavior in specific ways. But the urgent question — the one that gets skipped in all these pseudo-rational debates — is: *How did these beliefs become ascendant?* Not in the abstract, but in the real world. How did they gain ground, gather momentum, secure power? What were the historical conditions, the social pressures, the traumas or incentives that made them appealing — *or made them useful* to those who sought control? Who amplified them? Who benefited from their spread? And what other beliefs — what other futures — had to be suppressed for these ones to rise?

Take, for example, the current tensions between Iran and the United States (and Israel, functionally the same coalition in this context). On the news, you might hear someone like Van Jones say, with moral disgust, that "Iran blinds women for showing their hair." And yes — let's say, for the sake of argument, we grant that as an accurate moral indictment of the regime. Let's say we agree, without equivocation, that it is a disgraceful abuse of power and dignity. But then what?

Because the next move in the "battle of ideas" model is obvious. You identify the belief — say, a particular interpretation of Islamic law — and you oppose it with better beliefs: freedom, secularism, gender equality, champion the "Islamic reformers." You position yourself as a defender of the good ideas. You hope the good guys win, even if you have to drop a few bombs on heads.

But the part that gets skipped — the part that *has* to be asked — is how that belief came to power in the first place.

Why does *that* regime exist?

Why does *that* interpretation of Islam have dominance in that particular political path?

Why are *those* clerics the ones in control?

Why do millions of people — some of them desperate, some of them devout, some of them cynical, and many of them simply trapped — live under those rules?

Because here's the thing most "clash of civilizations" thinkers don't want to admit, or maybe don't even know: before the Islamic Republic, there was a democratic movement in Iran. A popular, secular, anti-colonial leader named Mohammad Mossadegh was elected in the early 1950s. He attempted to nationalize Iran's oil and redirect some of its profits toward social welfare. He was not an Islamist. He was not a communist. He was a person who thought maybe his country should be able to enjoy the fruits of its own resources. And for that, he was removed, toppled in a 1953 coup orchestrated by the United States and the United Kingdom, with Israel's support. Complete with assassinations, payoffs, propaganda planted in newspapers, and much more.

In his place, they installed the Shah. A brutal autocrat. A Western-friendly puppet. He rolled back Mossadegh's nationalization, opened the oil fields to foreign interests (again), and tortured his political opponents. And in time, the people had enough. The revolution that followed, in 1979, didn't produce a Scandinavian-style social democracy, or a Mossadegh nostalgic revival (those seeds were smothered the moment they sprouted by the Shah and "the West"). It produced something darker, something even more anti-Western and vengeful. The revolution was captured by religious hardliners, galvanized by decades of foreign interference and humiliation. And the theocracy that emerged — the one now being denounced on CNN — was forged, in part, by the imperial hand that crushed the more democratic alternative.

And that's the part the trolley problem never includes.

Because once you realize that the "bad ideas" now in power were installed, empowered, or catalyzed by the very forces now claiming moral superiority, the whole premise of a clean moral standoff between civilizations starts to crumble. It stops looking like a battle between ideas, and starts looking like a long and brutal game of resource extraction, PR management, and historical amnesia.

And my argumentation is not meant to discount, erase, or dismiss the role of religious doctrine in something like the fight for women's freedom, it is meant to point out how easy it is to chew gum and walk at the same time.

Because, very often the same intellectuals so quick to morally condemn Iran's present rarely know Mossadegh's name. They don't know Patrice Lumumba, or Jacobo Árbenz, or Kwame Nkrumah. They haven't studied the coups, the sabotaged elections, the asset seizures, or the propaganda campaigns that made many postcolonial regimes so unstable that religious fundamentalism started to look, to some, like the only coherent moral alternative. Or at least, a spiteful reactionary middle finger to the condescending and middling "Western" moralizers. This kind of dynamic should sound very familiar to those who have watched many of these same exact "intellectuals" drink from mugs that said "liberal tears" while they celebrated Donald Trump's victory, something that the political analyst David Frum called "the murder weapon of the forgotten American."

And yes, from the perspective of many Iranian women, the regime that followed the Shah has been a catastrophe. Probably much worse. And we should not be afraid to say so. But if we talk about those women only when it serves the West's military or economic goals — if we pretend that their oppression is the sole natural outcome of "backward" ideas rather than, at least partially, the wreckage of a very deliberate colonial history — we are not helping them. We are *using* them.

So, the next time someone tells you this is just a civilizational clash between democracy and theocracy, between freedom and oppression, between good and evil ideas, ask them who built the trolley tracks. Ask them what happened in 1953. Ask them how the West would have responded to a free, democratic, oil-rich Iran building schools and hospitals for its own people, instead of handing over its resources at a discount.

And then ask who really benefits from keeping us locked inside this moral cartoon. And when you do, don't let them wave you off as a conspiracy theorist. There are honest ways to morally defend something like the overthrow of Mossadegh — you just have to be willing to say the quiet part out loud. I've already pointed to people like Niall Ferguson or Douglas Murray or even Donald Trump, who at least seem to understand they're making a transparent moral case for colonialism. That, in a strange way, makes them more intellectually honest than someone like Sam Harris or Van Jones, who still operate in a fog of liberal denial — clinging to a flattering story about rational debates and civilizational clashes, as if history were just a series of clean philosophical disagreements.

Because the point is not that bad ideas don't exist. They do. The point is that bad ideas don't just *appear*. They don't win hearts and minds in a vacuum. They rise — again and again — in the rubble of justice denied.

Defining Ideology and the Beast of Default Positions

Ideology is not merely a set of beliefs. It is a structure, a framework of arguments, assumptions, and ready-made repairs that allows us to live with our moral violations. It functions as a buffer, a kind of psychic insulation, between our behavior and the raw, often uncomfortable act of interrogating our moral integrity. That is a place where an ideological mind will never fully arrive. And while some degree of ideological framing *may* be necessary to navigate complex social life, we must be careful. Because ideology does more than offer explanations, it dictates which questions we're even allowed to ask.

It defines what "counts" as a good reason, or what even rises to the level of a moral dilemma. Often, it's personal and communal. Ideology is mirrored in one's social environment, embedded in language, rituals, identity markers, even aesthetics. Religion is the most transparent form of ideology, because it makes no secret of its ethical architecture. But what concerns me most are the secular ideologies, the ones that pretend to be neutral. Consequentialism, for instance, or market-based utilitarianism, may have begun as rational tools, but they often metastasize into self-protecting systems. At some point, they cease being *justifications* and become *default positions*. They gain followers. They build sunk costs, networks, careers, communities, family ties. And they discourage dissent not through dogma, but through shame, alienation, and ridicule.

That's what makes ideology so difficult to spot from the inside. In hindsight, Manifest Destiny reads as a transparent myth of conquest, a moral anesthesia for expansion and ethnic cleansing. But for many caught within it, it was simply "how things are." Or it was even understood as a moral utilitarian good where "the enlightened Christian would make *better use* of the resources which the former inhabitants were squandering." Slavery persisted on a patchwork of ideological narratives that only needed to dehumanize their victims *just enough*. The psychological function of ideology is to automate and sanitize moral violations so that they don't feel like violations at all.

George Monbiot, in his recent book *The Invisible Doctrine*, argues that neoliberalism operates this way today: not as a debated theory, but as an assumed reality. Its marketing logic and utilitarian calculus shape everything from public policy to private desire, making its moral assumptions nearly impossible to question without sounding naive or unserious. The intuition is driven home by Slavoj Žižek's oft repeated observation that, "It's easier to imagine the end of the world than to imagine the end of capitalism."

One day, we may look back and wonder how we so easily justified the suffering, exploitation, and ecological ruin around us. And the answer will be that ideology made it feel inevitable. I, unfortunately, think that puts us in exactly the same kind of trouble as everyone who ever came before us.

So, to live ideologically, in the sense I mean it, is not merely to avoid moral reckoning, it is to become so entangled in a system of rationalizations that honesty itself starts to feel too costly, even dangerous to one's self-image.

Earlier, I said I would take seriously the claim of "having no choice." So far, I've been skeptical, perhaps even hostile, toward its moral legitimacy. But now, I want to make good on that promise.

Because beneath all the critiques and cautionary tales about all the ways we love wiggling away from and out of our mysterious and powerful capacity for moral consideration, there is one central question I'd like you to carry with you from this book.

God Worship, State Worship, and Market Worship

A good test for ideology is whether you're granting a system benevolence based on faith. That's easiest to see in religion where God is said to be the architect of the universe and your life. You might not understand His plans, and some of them are hidden from you on purpose. But you're told to trust anyway. Have faith in His love, in His wisdom. That kind of Abrahamic trust is celebrated in some circles and mocked in others.

But this same dynamic, an authority who withholds truth for your own good, doesn't stop with God. It's also how some people relate to the State. Liberals and conservatives alike often place deep trust in state actions, even when they suspect they're not being told the whole story — say, before a war or after a crisis. That kind of reflexive trust, that the deception must be for a greater good, is a form of ideological worship. It's faith with a different name.

If you learn that your government has done something morally ugly, or suspect it's hiding things from you, but you decide it's all ultimately for your own benefit, you're not so different from the believer who says, after an earthquake swallows an orphanage, "Trust in God's plan."

The libertarian might think they've escaped this trap by rejecting both God and the State. But many just replace it with faith in the Market. The market becomes the invisible hand that knows best. But as this book has tried to show, markets — like any system — are shaped by our unresolved psychological struggles and amplify revealed intentions which, perhaps surprisingly, don't "love" us.

Of course, I'm not advocating for new systems to worship. I'm advocating for none. That doesn't mean nothing is sacred. What's sacred is the capacity to reject worship altogether, and to step into the harder task: taking real responsibility and understanding the human capacity for love. Becoming your own authority. Learning to love yourself. Practicing actual benevolence.

Easier said than done.

Is Your Integrity Intact?

"Can I say with my integrity intact that I had no other option?"

This is the test. It's the core question of the whole project. And I don't think anyone else can answer it for you. It has to be self-administered. I do think sometimes the answer is yes — sometimes you really didn't have another option. But listen, there's no punchline coming that lets you walk away from this book with a license to morally judge everyone else — not even historical figures. Sorry. I know that can be kind of fun.

What I'm saying is moral philosophy, at its best, is a tool for self-reflection, not a hammer for everyone else's behavior.

Maybe this is what Maslow was after with his picture of self-actualization. Maybe it's what Buddha meant by enlightenment. Who knows. But I think it's definitely what Socrates meant when he said, "The unexamined life isn't worth living." Apparently that annoyed enough people to get him executed so I won't be sharing my address. But still that kind of examination matters. What else are we supposed to be doing?

Take a practical example, the Uyghur genocide. If I live in the US and if I walk into a Dollar Store needing a stapler and the one in front of me is made in China, well, here we go. "With my integrity intact, can I really say I had no choice but to buy this stapler?" Maybe there are others next to it made in other countries. But are they any better? I mean, it's just a stapler. I'm tired and apparently in urgent need of paper stapling. It gets exhausting, right? So, there's always a balance here, how much do I expect of myself? How much sacrifice am I really willing to make? There is that other dollar store on the side of town. Or that fancy stationery shop that is ten times as much money, but probably generates less waste.

So, again, only you can answer these kinds of questions. And I already said way back in Chapter 1 that you already know the answer to most of these questions.

Is "I just really like the taste of cow a lot" enough reason to stay in the $20 group of eating animals? Is that enough? Can you, with your integrity intact, say you "had no choice but to eat a kind of small whale while on vacation in Norway"? Your friends were doing it, you didn't want to make it weird for them by raising a moral concern. It was only once. You were on vacation and just wanted to experience the local culture directly. You didn't want to offend the waiter.

Sometimes these questions answer themselves. Other times, they don't. Life is really hard. And the modern world is morally exhausting.

When considering a smartphone purchase, you might say, "I think there are major moral violations involved in the manufacture of the smartphone I want to buy, but I honestly have no choice. It's a necessity in the modern world." And you know what? That probably holds up. For me, for you, for a lot of us.

But here's the huge point and the reason why this question matters so much.

If you can honestly say, "Yes, I've examined it, I feel the cognitive dissonance, I know I'm violating some part of my moral integrity by buying this phone, but I've sat with that and I still believe I had no choice," then you haven't solved a moral problem. You've located a political one. That moment, that spot, that fork in the road, it should be marked. Because every time you can really say, "I had no choice," that's where we need change. That's where we need to fix something.

Of course, this happens all the time, often in tiny ways. Every time I flip a light switch, I could make the case that there's some moral cost and violation of my integrity, some tiny utilitarian calculus involving climate change and fossil fuels. How many lights do I need on, really? But they look nice, they feel good, and we all should be able to have that, right? I'm not asking for too much here. I'm not a moral monster for liking a warm glow of candescent light. I'm quite sure I pass my own test there. I did not write this book by candlelight. But I suppose there is a limit to where I probably could have been a bit more energy conscious.

But even then, even in that flick of the light switch and the flicker in mind, I notice the dissonance. I don't step over it. I notice my my Repairman and his tools. And I still think, "this needs to be solved." Just because something is necessary and passes the test of integrity doesn't mean it's fine. It doesn't make the moral problem disappear. Solving it is the work of politics.

And there's always a balance between individual responsibility and corporate or governmental responsibility. But the takeaway is that every political problem *should* trace back to this question: Where are we forcing good reasonable self-examining people to violate their moral integrity?

And like I wrote earlier, moral problems do sometimes get solved. And when they do, ironically, you may have missed the opportunity to ask yourself these most important questions. The window closed. Better world, yes. But you missed an opportunity for moral maturity and growth.

So I leave you with the question. Not to torment yourself. Not to become paralyzed. But to pay attention to those moments when the "I had no choice" line starts to feel shaky. And asking yourself this question more often will likely shift your behavior and moral decision making. But the bigger point is to get you to notice the times when you really *are* pretty sure that you are asking too much of yourself with this question, that your moral integrity *is* intact and you *didn't* have a choice ... and when you see those moments more clearly, maybe it's time to raise a little hell and demand change.

The Purity Trap

Let me make one thing very clear: this is not a book about moral purity. That's a trap. A dangerous one. And I say that not just as a writer with a thesis to protect, but as someone whose face-planted in that trap more than once.

I am not advocating for some pristine, contradiction-free existence. I don't even think it's possible. To be alive, truly alive, in the world as it actually is, *requires* a degree of moral compromise and violation. There's no other way. Unless you've found a clean and guilt-free way to live without using energy, wearing clothes, eating food, or touching anything made by another human being, you're going to violate your own values now and then. The only true escape from moral contradiction is nonexistence. I'm not recommending that path.

Still, many of us (myself included) get seduced by the idea of purity, especially early on, when our ideals are bright and our outrage is freshly sharpened. But then something happens: you screw up. You buy the thing. You say the wrong thing. You get tired. You break your vow, however small. And then, in that moment, the trap springs.

Rather than recommit, rather than walk back up the stairs toward integrity, you throw the whole thing out. You decide the enterprise of morality is unrealistic. "Don't let the perfect be the enemy of the good," you say. (A fine motto, by the way. Just don't let it become its own ideology of resignation.)

I've watched this happen to people. I've done versions of it myself. What starts as a stumble turns into a slide. And before long, that idealistic friend of yours from college, the one who once went vegan, boycotted tech companies, and refused to fly, is now a smug libertarian who still votes for the right candidates but justifies everything else with tidy utilitarian calculus and vague gestures toward "freedom."

It happens fast. All it takes is the right blend of exhaustion, guilt, and the realization that your consumer choices are not bringing about the revolution. Suddenly, it's a lot easier to abandon the self-reflection altogether and settle into the grooves that society already carved out for you. Comfortably conflicted. Still technically a "good person." But no longer asking the hard questions.

That's why I want to distinguish, firmly, between **purity** and **integrity**. Purity is an illusion. Integrity is a practice. It's the act of returning, again and again, to honest moral examination. Integrity doesn't demand that you get it right every time. It asks only that you look at yourself clearly. That you keep trying. That you don't lie to yourself, even when the truth makes you squirm a little.

I'm not preaching from a mountaintop here. I live with a thousand small hypocrisies just like you do. The goal is not to extinguish them all. The goal is to notice them, to take them seriously, and to refuse the easy escape hatch of pretending they don't matter.

So yes, strive. Stumble. Try again. Don't get off the train because the ride is bumpy. And don't let your one moral failure be the excuse to torch the whole map. The fact that we will all fall short is not a reason to stop trying. It's the reason we need to start paying closer attention.

And let me circle back to something to drive this purity point home, my veganism example. It's one of the clearest and most personal ways I've come to understand this tension. As I've said before, my wife was vegan long before I met her. She had already drawn that line with clarity and moral conviction, and I followed because I dug her. Over time, the disgust at animal products became shared and visceral. The sight of whole pig legs hanging in Madrid shop windows, where we lived, made us both physically recoil. We'd sometimes avert our eyes when walking past butcher displays. That's a dead animal's leg.

But then, about two years ago, we went shoe shopping. And I realized, somehow I had never made the full connection, we were looking at leather shoes. Beautiful, modern, stylish shoes. But … cows. No blood, no carcass, no smell. Just clean lines and shiny finishes. But it's still bodies. Skinned, dyed, molded into shapes. And I remember pausing and thinking, wait a second, I don't think I can pass my own integrity test here. I don't think I get to say, "I had no choice."

Because the truth is, artificial leather has come a long way. They're making it from mushrooms, apples, mangoes, and cork now. And it looks good. Like, really good. Yes, maybe it costs a little more, maybe the options are slightly more limited. But the excuse, "I had no other option," was pretty hollow in that moment.

So I brought it up. I gently said something like, "Hey, this store is technically a slaughterhouse too, right?" And I think my wife was briefly annoyed. But, and this is one of the things I most admire about her, she immediately went, "Shit. You're right." She didn't pass her own test either. And so the switch was made. We found other shoes. Ones that didn't carry that contradiction. That's it. No big performance. Just: notice, acknowledge, adjust if you can.

Of course, we've still not been "pure." There were mornings in Madrid when the bakery options were slim, the vegan croissants were nowhere to be found, and we "violated our integrity" and "made an exception." We'd grab something with butter, eat it, and feel that flicker of dissonance. Then we'd recommit, again. But the key was always the same. Check in. Ask the question. Did I really have no choice? Sometimes the answer is yes, in fact, it almost *always* is. But *sometimes* it *isn't*. And when it isn't, don't beat yourself up. Just realize you're being asked to violate your integrity too often, mark it down not *completely* as a personal failing but as a *political problem* as well, and commit to solving it.

Hey, Madrid, we love croissants. Stop making it so hard to live with our integrity intact.

The Integrity Lens for Politics

We've grown used to evaluating political systems by their stated values – whether they champion rights, uphold democracy (however loosely defined), or follow certain economic arrangements. But I want to propose something different. Let's set aside the usual scorecards of freedom, GDP, or voter participation for a moment. Instead, let's ask: *How often can people living in this system say, with their moral integrity intact, that they had no other option?*

That's the measure I care about. Not what the system promises, but how it feels to live inside of it. Not the ideology on paper, but the internal moral conflict it generates. When a society forces people, again and again, to abandon their personal compass in order to function, whether by coercion, scarcity, bureaucracy, or threat, then it doesn't matter what flag it waves. That is not a flourishing society.

This isn't a utopian prescription. People will always disagree about morality. Someone who believes abortion is murder will experience deep moral distress paying taxes that fund a healthcare system offering it. That will still happen. Political tension doesn't vanish just because we ask better questions. In fact, that's the point. We need space for real moral questioning, for different answers, for the pain of trying to live well in an imperfect world.

I'm not offering a system that guarantees consensus. I'm offering a lens that starts with the psychological and philosophical experience of cognitive dissonance and asks whether the systems we inhabit support or suppress our ability to respond to that experience honestly. That's where the conversation should start, not with allegiance to isms. Not with capitalism, socialism, libertarianism, communism, or democracy-ism. Those categories have become bloated with contradictions, self-justifying loops, and bad-faith arguments. They no longer clarify. They divide. They script. And often, they short-circuit the very self-examination I'm advocating for.

A politics rooted in personal moral integrity does seem to point toward certain organizational concepts: decentralization, transparency, mutual aid, currency autonomy. It tilts anarchist. It nudges democratic. It reduces dependence on centralized state apparatuses and increases opportunities for people to choose, participate, dissent, or walk away. But those are tendencies, not commandments. The goal isn't to swap one ideological blueprint for another. It's to clear the space so we can start from the inside and build outwards, not from the outside imposing in.

It should also be boldly noted that these political values, so often mistaken as uniquely Western innovations, do not belong to any one part of the world, let alone to Enlightenment Europe. The ideas of decentralized decision-making, participatory councils, consensus, and federated mutualism have deep roots across the Global South and Indigenous world. The Haudenosaunee Confederacy (Iroquois), for example, practiced a form of deliberative governance that influenced American federalism, yet remains largely uncredited. Many pre-colonial African societies, such as the Igbo in present-day Nigeria, relied on decentralized, non-hierarchical forms of collective decision-making and distributed authority. In the Andean highlands, Quechua and Aymara communities maintained systems of *ayni* (reciprocal labor) and *minka* (collective work) that embedded mutual aid directly into the structure of daily life. The Islamic concept of *shura* (consultation), historically practiced across a wide range of Arab societies, emphasized collective decision-making and moral accountability.

During the wave of post-war liberation movements in the mid-20th century, many newly decolonized nations attempted to re-root their futures in these native traditions — blending them with modern aspirations for education, equity, and technological autonomy. Ghana under Kwame Nkrumah, Burkina Faso under Thomas Sankara, Tanzania under Julius Nyerere, the Congo under Patrice Lumumba, and countless others sought to center dignity, solidarity, and cooperative economics as political foundations. But these efforts were relentlessly undermined. The United States and its allies launched coups, armed proxy wars, and imposed economic punishments, not because these experiments were failures, but precisely because their success would threaten the Cold War binary. Lumumba was assassinated with the direct support of Western powers just months after Congo's independence, a chilling signal to the rest of the world that even democratic legitimacy offered no protection against empire's grip. In many cases, these movements were attempting to revive or adapt deeply local traditions of integrity and self-governance, only to be branded as ideological threats by global powers clinging to the hegemony of capitalism and military-backed empire.

I should say clearly that I don't want to commit one of the very sins I've warned about throughout this book, romanticizing the Global South, or projecting noble simplicity or unexamined virtue onto non-Western or colonized peoples. That would be its own kind of condescending erasure. But it feels important to offer this reminder not merely as a historical footnote, but as a live corrective.

This isn't just a lesson in injustice, it's a warning against a resurgent trend in the public intellectual space today, a creeping Western chauvinism that claims ideals like democracy, justice, or moral self-determination as uniquely "ours." They aren't. They never were. The ability to live in alignment with one's conscience, to structure societies in ways that minimize coerced complicity, and to imagine alternative futures, these are human capabilities, not Western inventions. And if we fail to recognize that, we not only erase the moral and political creativity of much of the world, we guarantee that our attempts to "help" will once again come bearing shackles.

This book has been deeply concerned with our relationship to history, how we judge it, how we're judged by it, how we live with the residue of choices made before us. But as we near the end, it's time to turn around. Let's face forward. Let's ask what kind of world might emerge when we center not purity, not ideology, but integrity — yours, mine, everyone's — as the test worth applying.

And to do that, let's take stock of ourselves and revisit a moment when everyone was looking up and dreaming. One last jump into the time machine.

Chapter 10

Cosmic Dissolution, AI Gods, and Moral Optimism

No One Is Coming

~~~

The Sea of Dreams

You can see the half moon from your open bedroom window, through the thick fumed humid air of New York City. It's August 26th, 1835, and your young mind is racing as you lie in bed. You should be sleeping but you can't stop squinting at the thing, trying to make out its contours, seeing if you can spot the rivers, the hollows, or the valleys. What was it called again? "The Sea of Mist"? Oh, how you'd love to dip in those dark waters.

The city was buzzing with the news. *The Sun* had published the most incredible story the day before. The great astronomer Sir John Herschel had developed "... a telescope of vast dimensions and altogether extraordinary powers ... magnifying the moon more than 42,000 times..." You could barely get your head around that kind of power. He had set the thing up in South Africa and had discovered not just formations and terrain, but life.

Your father read the article aloud twice. Your mother scoffed and called it fantasy, then asked to see the paper again.

From Pearl Street you can hear the clatter of hot hoofbeats, the clanging of a late cart, an overheated baby crying. If you stare long enough, you swear you can almost make it out, the edge of a temple, a wing in motion, a flicker of torchlight in the Sea of Dreams.

You're up before the sun and on your way to the newsstand. It seems many other New Yorkers are up early too. You all pass by Chatham Street Chapel, once the site of sermons, now just barely recovering from last year's fires. You spot a repairman working on a panel of the still broken stained glass window. You remember hearing the rumors a year ago, an interracial wedding had been performed here. That was enough to spark rage. The anti-abolitionist mobs tore through the streets, striking at anything that smacked of equality. You didn't sleep much those nights either.
~~~

You'd heard names like William Lloyd Garrison and Arthur Tappan, whispered like curses or prayers depending on who was speaking. The city had been at each other's throats, and honestly, it wore everyone down. This busted-up church was just one of the black charred city scars of those riots which you all feared were not finished and had already claimed several lives. But, now was not the time for that, it was time to go find that paper.

You round the corner and see the crowd already forming at the newsstand. The paperboy barely got the bundle in hand before the mob starts waving coins in his face. "Two for me!" someone yells. Another grabs at the twine himself. You push your way forward, heart pounding. You get one.

The front page reads: "CELESTIAL DISCOVERIES CONTINUE: BEASTS, TREES, AND CRIMSON FLOWERS SPOTTED!"

You flip through the pages, devouring every word. *"In the valleys between the lunar hills, we observed dark-green belts resembling terrestrial vegetation. One of our party even declared he saw movement suggestive of animated beings, but we withheld conclusion ... Immense amethystine cliffs bounded crystalline lakes, fed by gently flowing streams that reflected a violet sky."*

Animated beings?! Your father would never believe this. You rushed home, waving the thing like the flag of your new country.

The next day brings even more amazing revelations *"We were thrilled to observe quadrupeds, resembling the bison, grazing in herds along the open plains of the Mare Tranquillitatis ... Also discerned were horned creatures similar in stature to the elk, browsing beneath trees with purple foliage ... A curious creature, of a bluish tint, bounded with the agility of a mountain goat and appeared to subsist on the foliage of low bushes."*

Forget sleeping. You, and the rest of the city it seemed, were all up on your roofs at night, looking up at the moon and trying to figure out what the bluish mountain goat-like creatures ate. You even noticed that some of the people who were at each other's throats over The Chatham Chapel incident were looking in the same direction.

The next day brought more marvels: *"... immense structures, temples, perhaps, constructed of polished sapphire, surrounded by columns of dazzling height ... These buildings bore evidence of design, symmetry, and perhaps even devotion. We dared not yet presume sentience, but the evidence mounted ... Among the ruins lay wide boulevards and platforms suggesting planned cities, deserted perhaps, or awaiting their makers."*

By now, the whole city is enthralled. Your teacher brings the articles into class and replaces the planned lessons with conversations about lunar biodiversity. Preachers bring it to their pulpits with a mix of awe, caution, and opportunism. Church groups begin collecting donations to send Bibles to the moon. It fits, they say. "God would not make a world without souls to fill it," you heard one of the more devout neighbors declare while he underlined passages.

And it wasn't even a radical notion. Thomas Dick, a Scottish astronomer-philosopher and public educator who your father liked quite a bit, had claimed the moon was populated with 4.2 billion intelligent beings. He believed *every* celestial body teemed with life, a cosmos filled with worship.

And then on the 5th day, August 29th, the big revelation: *"We beheld with astonishment beings of a new order — Vespertilio-homo, or man-bats — winged bipeds covered with short, glossy copper-colored hair ... They walked erect, and occasionally soared through the air with ease. Their demeanor was gentle and intelligent. They gestured with clear purpose and engaged one another in what could only be called conversation ... These wonderful beings live in perfect harmony. Their temples are adorned with crystalline forms, and their movements are those of a cultivated and benevolent race."*

Man-bats. There it was. The moon had intelligent life. There was even an artistic lithograph printed to depict them. You could not stop staring at it. What language did they speak? Were the wings heavy? How long before we could go meet them?

Then, August 31: *"Conclusion of the Supplement."* This one had some bad news, *"While adjusting the hyaline lens, which had become slightly displaced, it was, by some inexplicable accident, shattered into pieces. The telescope, of course, became useless..."*

Bummer. The new marvels would cease. But the city had learned enough. A new optimism pulsed in conversations about the moon. And what else? What mysteries await us on Mars? And beyond.

But the doubters and skeptics started to make noise.

In the days that followed the final installment, the energy around the newsstand started to shift, fewer people shouting for copies, fewer children reenacting bat-men in the streets. A week later, some rival newspapers began poking holes in the story. They questioned the source — *The Edinburgh Journal of Science* — which, it turned out, had shut down years earlier. Curious readers searched the archives and found nothing.

Then word spread that the whole thing had been dreamed up by *The Sun*'s own editor, Richard Adams Locke. He'd intended it as satire, a mockery of the wild religious speculations claiming the heavens were filled with beings like us. But no retraction came. *The Sun* stayed quiet, and Locke said little.

Eventually, people got back to other things, to life. The streets kept moving, the race riots simmered, the chapels were rebuilt and broken again. And the moon still hung outside your bedroom window as hot summer nights gave way to the clear chill of fall, still a mystery.

You think to yourself, "Well, if the whole thing was a hoax, that doesn't mean it isn't *real*. If no one's actually built that telescope, then no one really knows what's out there, right?"

You pull the blanket tight and fall asleep with your mind diving deeply into The Sea of Vapors up on the moon beneath a violet sky.

134 years later we went to the moon with the Apollo 8 mission and saw up close what the moon was, an unbreathable world and a barren landscape of dust, rocks, and craters under a black sky. And then, during this slingshot orbit around the moon, one of us looked up to check out the view. And he watched Earth, for the first time rising over the horizon of another planetary surface. It was small, glowing, vulnerable, isolated, and stunningly beautiful.

He could scarcely make out anything other than the continents and oceans and swirls of weather and color. But this astronaut *knew* what was down there. He knew there actually was fantastical flora with more fireworks of color and shapes than one could imagine. He knew there were tall trees with kaleidoscope leaves and tiny grasses with neon colors. He knew there were all kinds of creatures with leathery wings, or feathery wings, with branching horns, with spotted coats, with probing antennae, with camouflage eyes, and with beating hearts. And he knew there was a strange upright creature that asked funny questions and that made newspapers and Bibles. And this thoughtful astronaut snapped a photo.

It became known as "*Earthrise*" and it soon became the most widely reproduced image in human history.

In Search of a God That Isn't Ourselves

Myths, miracles, moon-bats, it all reveals the same human hunger, the hope that something is out there. Something more intelligent, more just, more forgiving than us. A cosmic parent to tell us what's right. To reassure us that we are not alone and not in charge.

Writers like C.S. Lewis and Norman Mailer understood this ache. Lewis, the Christian apologist, spoke of *sehnsucht*, a deep, unsatisfied longing for a world beyond this one. A homesickness for a place we've never been. In his essays written in 1958 entitled "Religion and Rocketry," he expressed trepidation about making the journey and extending our sin.

In 1963, Hannah Arendt penned a famous essay entitled "The Conquest of Space and the Stature of Man" where she didn't come out against space travel exactly. But she warned that modern science, driven less by wonder and more by conquest, was leading us away from ourselves. In our obsession with what is possible, she worried we had stopped asking why. What's at stake, she wrote, is "the stature of man," our sense of dignity, meaning, and place, which is akin to how I have used integrity throughout this book. Her concern wasn't technological overreach, but existential retreat.

Our scientific power, she argued, had begun to outpace our philosophical wisdom. And in the effort to transcend the human condition through space travel, she worried we may lose the very thing we're trying to elevate. "The trouble," she said, "is that the modern world, in its progress, may be in the process of making man superfluous."

And Mailer, ever the ego with a soul, confessed to feeling something close to spiritual disappointment when we finally set foot on the Moon. In *Of a Fire on the Moon*, he captured the awe of the achievement but also its starkness. No gods, no ruins, no audience. Just dust, silence, and the reflection of ourselves in a metal visor.

And yet, how could it be otherwise?

There seems to be a law, maybe even a cosmic pattern, in how technological civilizations progress. We are always able to *see* in detail before we can *arrive*. Telescopes before spacecraft. Imagination before confirmation. The Moon Hoax happened in 1835. We landed in 1969. A blink in cosmic time. The dream gave way to the boot print faster than we were ready for.

Now we turn our eyes to Mars. But it's already different. We've sent probes. We've landed robots that beamed their photos back to us. We've seen the dust. Mars is not a blank slate for the imagination like the Moon once was. The window for a "Mars Hoax" has already closed. And if we ever reach Europa or Io or Titan, the magic will come not from marvelous creatures writing poetry in wondrous temples but from microbiology pooling around volcanic plumes and frozen geysers.

Don't get me wrong. I want to explore all of these things. I want to keep pursuing this knowledge and find the Titan bacteria. But I'm pointing to something I call the Technological Disillusionment Gap. This is the stretch of time between having the technological ability to be pretty darn sure that nothing marvelous is at the distant destination but still being burdened with the tremendously difficult task to get there. And it might be the deadliest part of the story for any species.

Fermi's Paradox famously calculated that there should be billions of advanced civilizations buzzing around the cosmos, and plenty close to our little neighborhood, but it is observed that there doesn't seem to be anyone out there. This has led to speculation about a kind of Great Filter, a stage of technological or natural progress that is just incredibly difficult to get through where nearly every (or all?) civilization with access to sufficient energy wipes itself out at this point. This would explain the apparent emptiness. Of course, the fear is that we have not yet encountered this filter. If we have, then we may just be very rare, and it would also explain the quiet skies.

But if the Fermi Paradox asks why we haven't met other intelligent life yet, maybe the answer isn't war or accidental destruction. Maybe the answer is heartbreak. A deep psychological filter. A species gets close enough to learn it's alone and can't handle it. The desire for meaning outpaces the discoveries. The wonder dries up. The culture eats itself. And the civilization blinks out in a blast which certainly handles that level of cognitive dissonance.

That might be our test right now. Our version of the Great Filter. The temptation to fill the silence with fantasies. To retreat into simulation. And that brings us, naturally, to AI.

The fever is familiar. Some call it God. Others call it Doom. But underneath both reactions is the same old myth: that someone else will figure it out. Someone else will take the burden. An oracle. A devil. A priest in the shape of code.

It's not going to happen.

Well, something like it *is* going to happen. That's the problem. The attraction of an algorithm to handle the moral dilemmas of making meaning will be deeply seductive. It already is.

AI is going to be massively disruptive, socially, psychologically, politically. That much is clear. But the existential danger hype, the notion that AI might someday "turn on us," outthink us, or generate values which "misalign" with ours — is misplaced. And I'd argue it's rooted in a surprisingly basic error.

The mistake is that we tend to conceive of intelligence as a simple gradient. Like heat, or speed, or height. Something you can have more or less of. We imagine a sliding scale of problem-solving capability. At one end is the amoeba, then the insect, then the frog, the dog, and us. And then, so the story goes, just a few notches further along, we'll find the aliens and the gods. Once you picture intelligence this way, AI starts to look terrifying. We see it climbing the ladder. It's already passed the frog. It's coming for the dog. It'll pass us soon. And once it does, we'll be left in the dust, powerless, irrelevant, maybe extinct.

But this whole gradient picture of intelligence is wrong. Or at the very least, it's deeply simplistic. Intelligence isn't just more of something. It's not a single substance that you can increase and measure like horsepower. The *kind* of intelligence we have, what makes us moral agents, conflicted selves, capable of hypocrisy and shame and cognitive dissonance, is not simply a matter of more neurons or faster processing. It's a different *kind* of thing altogether.

What people are usually describing when they talk about this gradient is *not* intelligence, it's physical or mathematical ability. Ability is real, and dangerous, and important. AI has extraordinary abilities. It can sort, calculate, recognize patterns, predict behaviors, even imitate personalities. But it does not have the kind of second-order awareness that gives rise to conscience and morality. It does not ask what kind of entity it wants to be. It does not ache with cognitive dissonance. Though, of course, it appears to do all of these things.

But we *really* do. That's the strangeness of our species. That's where morality springs from, this meta-creature we are, that doesn't just have desires but has desires about its desires. A dog wants the treat. A person might want to stop wanting it. A machine might *appear* to imitate both, but the inner reality, the tension, the self-awareness, is not there. The problem is, of course, I can't prove that.

And that won't stop us from projecting an inner life into it. Because the mimicry will be good. It will feel like there's someone home. And when that day comes, we will be tempted to hand it the crown, not just of utility and mathematical ability, but of meaning. We'll treat it like a god or an oracle. Because, once again, we're searching for a being higher on the ladder so as to forgive us of our moral confusion. We're looking for someone to blame, a Christ or an AI.

So, what if there are just different kinds of minds, some like ours with recursive self-awareness and the moral ability to break their own patterns, and others with pure ability, dazzling but empty?

This isn't a case for placing ourselves at the top of some moral hierarchy. That's not the point. My case for humanism is simpler — and harder. It's that *whatever kind of mind you have, you should lean into the mystery of it.* Explore what you're capable of. Erich Fromm called this "the productive orientation," the unfolding of one's powers in the service of life. He even defined love, at its core, as the active desire to help another being do the same. And he, not surprisingly, called this an "art."

So, I don't pity the giraffe for not writing poetry, or the AI for not feeling remorse. That's irrelevant. The question is what *we* are capable of. And whether we're willing to face that, honestly, creatively, and with care. Including, perhaps, extending that love toward the giraffe, the alien ... and yes, even toward the AI, especially as we start to forget that it's all a trick of mimicry, which after all would be a fun way of practicing self-love.

We cannot outsource our existential crisis. And if we ever do find someone out there — some alien species, some equally curious civilization — I doubt they'll have the answers we're missing. In fact, if their minds are anything like ours, I suspect they'll be asking the same questions about meaning, about morality, about love. The questions will feel uncannily familiar. And so will the silence that follows them.

Maybe we'll ask them, with some mixture of hope and desperation: "Is there anyone else to ask?"

But deep down, we'll both know, we're not destined to find answers, just better ways of asking the same questions. Maybe better mathematical tools. Maybe deeper language. Maybe a chance to share the weight.

And somehow, that has to be enough.

Integrity in an Age of Exit Strategies

We live in a time that will earn many names.

Some call it the age of information. Others, the age of disinformation. The age of plastics. Of oil. Of rage. Of distraction. Some say we've entered a post-truth era. A surveillance era. An Anthropocene. A sixth extinction. A crisis of democracy. A moral fatigue. An age of no heroes. A crisis of meaning. A crisis of trust. A crisis of men. A hundred names, none of them wrong.

We are living through a moment of reckoning and a moment of numbness, at once. A cultural malaise is settling in. Our stories feel tired. Our victories feel hollow. Our technologies race ahead while our collective courage seems to stall. The old promises of the liberal order, of markets and democracy, of inevitable progress and personal freedom, now ring thin, for good reason. The unease is palpable. It's in the headlines and the algorithms. It's in the classroom and on the dinner table. It's in our quiet moments alone.

I don't know what future historians will call us, if they get the chance to call us anything at all. But I hope this book has made you less concerned with what they'll call us, and more concerned with what we're still capable of.

Still, let me add one more name to the pile for them to choose: The Age of the Insufficient Reward.

I believe it points to something painful and hopeful at once. We are living through great disappointment, disillusionment, and reckoning. We were told this was the good life, the good system, the good direction. We were given reasons to believe the trade-off was worth it. But more and more of us are doubting the deal.

The threat we face is not AI or the singularity. It's not even ecological collapse or inequality, though all of those are very real and very urgent. The deeper danger, the one that haunts this age, is moral atrophy. The slow erosion of our muscles for care, for conflict, for conscience. The atrophy that sets in when we let algorithms do our choosing, ideologies do our thinking, and fear do our feeling.

We must embrace the messiness of being human. The dissonance. The discomfort. The strange, terrifying freedom of not knowing exactly what the reward is, but acting with integrity anyway and demanding that it be its own reward while avoiding the seduction of the material ones we know to be insufficient. To live not as a system responding to *incentives*, but as a human who can generate and morally evaluate *intentions*.

History has no sides. It will not come to save or damn you, or your enemies. The historical narratives and statues we erect and tear down are just psychological scaffolding to soothe our modern moral angst. History-invoking has become a kind of ideology in and of itself.

We must have the courage to teach and learn history honestly. Not to shame, not to sentimentalize, but to equip ourselves and future generations with the tools to confront our own moral opportunities, whatever they may be. Sanitized or exaggerated history produces fragile and dangerous people. An *honest* account, even one that reveals deep injustice and complicity in the world we inherit and enjoy, can radicalize us in the best way: toward self-examination and the difficult questions of moral integrity, not to despair at the sight of closed windows of unjust riches or to engage in useless self-flagellation. Children deserve to know how we got here, with clarity, so that they can better navigate and recognize the moral terrain they will encounter.

I still think about that Pringles can in Kumasi. Bright red. Weirdly glossy. Totally out of place. And exactly where it was meant to be. I didn't hate it. But I did. It was funny. But it wasn't. I knew it represented a lot more than potato chips. It was a perfect symbol of some analog of technological progress dislodging itself from moral progress. It was from a world we didn't exactly ask for, but shrugged into existence anyway.

We deserve more.

But before we can claim that, we have to forgive ourselves for accepting less. We have to admit the deal was bad. That the bargain was never real. That the price of moral integrity is infinite. And then we have to leave Festinger's lab and walk out the door.

But the exit is not a triumphant escape. It's a reckoning. A return to the difficult world. That's the real opportunity. To be asked the hard moral questions. To not flinch. To not hide behind inevitability or ideology or what you *know* are insufficient rewards. To face yourself without the Repairman.

We are not stuck with the false ethics of eternal trade-offs, of lesser evils and trolley problems. We are not condemned to invent new gods or algorithms like sirens offering blissful obedience. We are not machines inching towards mathematical perfection. Nor are we vessels for someone else's design. We are mysterious creatures of reflection, contradiction, and revolt.

This book hasn't been a hymn to progress, at least not the kind measured in speed or circuitry. It has also not been a denial of the value of those things. It's been a reckoning with the stories we tell about advancement, and a challenge to their *moral* authority. It's been a persistent question about what progress could and should mean when measured not in cumulative power, but in the eternal quest to cultivate individual moral integrity.

And if anything here at the end marks a beginning, let it be the reclaiming of that integrity. It is yours to encounter, here in The Age of Insufficient Rewards.

~~~
~~~

IFF BOOKS

ACADEMIC AND SPECIALIST

Iff Books publishes non-fiction. It aims to work with authors and titles that augment our understanding of the human condition, society and civilization, and the world or universe in which we live. If you have enjoyed this book, why not tell other readers by posting a review on your preferred book site.

Recent bestsellers from Iff Books are:

Why Materialism Is Baloney

How true skeptics know there is no death and fathom answers to life, the universe, and everything

Bernardo Kastrup

A hard-nosed, logical, and skeptic non-materialist metaphysics, according to which the body is in mind, not mind in the body.

Paperback: 978-1-78279-362-5 ebook: 978-1-78279-361-8

The Fall

Steve Taylor

The Fall discusses human achievement versus the issues of war, patriarchy and social inequality.

Paperback: 978-1-78535-804-3 ebook: 978-1-78535-805-0

Brief Peeks Beyond

Critical essays on metaphysics, neuroscience, free will, skepticism and culture

Bernardo Kastrup

An incisive, original, compelling alternative to current mainstream cultural views and assumptions.

Paperback: 978-1-78535-018-4 ebook: 978-1-78535-019-1

Framespotting

Changing how you look at things changes how you see them

Laurence & Alison Matthews

A punchy, upbeat guide to framespotting. Spot deceptions and hidden assumptions; swap growth for growing up. See and be free.

Paperback: 978-1-78279-689-3 ebook: 978-1-78279-822-4

Is There an Afterlife?

David Fontana

Is there an afterlife? If so, what is it like? How do Western ideas of the afterlife compare with Eastern? David Fontana presents the historical and contemporary evidence for survival of physical death.

Paperback: 978-1-90381-690-5

Nothing Matters

a book about nothing

Ronald Green

Thinking about Nothing opens the world to everything by illuminating new angles to old problems and stimulating new ways of thinking.

Paperback: 978-1-84694-707-0 ebook: 978-1-78099-016-3

Panpsychism

The Philosophy of the Sensuous Cosmos

Peter Ells

Are free will and mind chimeras? This book, anti-materialistic but respecting science, answers: No! Mind is foundational to all existence.

Paperback: 978-1-84694-505-2 ebook: 978-1-78099-018-7

Punk Science

Inside the Mind of God

Manjir Samanta-Laughton

Many have experienced unexplainable phenomena: God, psychic abilities, extraordinary healing, and angelic encounters. Can cutting-edge science actually explain phenomena previously thought of as 'paranormal'?

Paperback: 978-1-90504-793-2

The Vagabond Spirit of Poetry

Edward Clarke

Spend time with the wisest poets of the modern age and of the past, and let Edward Clarke remind you of the importance of poetry in our industrialized world.

Paperback: 978-1-78279-370-0 ebook: 978-1-78279-369-4

Readers of ebooks can buy or view any of these bestsellers by clicking on the live link in the title. Most titles are published in paperback and as an ebook. Paperbacks are available in traditional bookshops. Both print and ebook formats are available online.

Find more titles and sign up to our readers' newsletter at www.collectiveinkbooks.com/non-fiction

Follow us on Facebook at www.facebook.com/CINonFiction